TEMPTING TREATS

Canapés

I dedicate this book to my mother, who early on taught me the pleasures of cooking and enjoying delicious foods, and to my beloved daughters, Anna and Katarina, who follow a similar path.

ACKNOWLEDGEMENTS

I thank my assistants, Rachel and Susan, for their hard work and enthusiasm. I am also greatly indebted to the team of editor, designer, art director and last but not least photographer and assistant, who all helped to make the work on this book a wholly pleasurable experience.

TEMPTING TREATS

Canapés

Berit Vinegrad

OVER 100 COCKTAIL PARTY RECIPES

Little, Brown and Company

Boston   New York   Toronto   London

First U.S. Edition

ISBN 0-316-83123-9

10 9 8 7 6 5 4 3 2 1

Printed and bound in Singapore by Imago Productions Pte

Senior Editor: Joanna Lorenz
Art Director: Linda Cole
Art Editor: Muffy Dodson
Designer: Ingrid Mason
Photographer: Alan Newnham

CONTENTS

INTRODUCTION

The notion of cocktail parties conjures up images of sophisticated elegance, guests in evening finery, multi-coloured drinks in long-stemmed glasses and platters filled with delectable morsels of food. But as well as being glamorous and fun, the cocktail party is a practical way to entertain. Versatile enough to suit different occasions and times of day, it is also a fairly effortless way to give a party for a large number of guests, allowing a casual mix of friends and acquaintances seldom possible at dinner parties.

The food served at cocktail parties is of great importance though small in size. 'A piece of bread or toast with small savoury on top' is how the dictionary describes the canapé. A modest definition indeed of traditional cocktail party fare and the pretty, mouthwatering delicacies featured on the pages ahead. But as well as being visually delightful and a treat for the taste buds, a perfect canapé has some essentially practical features. It can be picked up with the fingers, whether self-contained as in the case of filled fruits and vegetables, threaded onto cocktail sticks or served inside some form of wrapping, and does not leave fingers sticky and greasy. It is small enough to be eaten in a mouthful or two at the most, and if eaten in two, it does not disintegrate with the first bite. If served hot, it is at a comfortable temperature.

When planning food for a cocktail party, bear a few things in mind. In terms of variety, five to six different types of canapé are sufficient and two pieces of each per head is enough. Conveniently, quite a few of the recipes here are suitable for freezing and can be baked straight from frozen, just before serving. A number can also be prepared well in advance, cling-filmed and refrigerated until needed. Others are more tricky and can only be partially prepared, and a few need to be freshly cooked.

When selecting your canapés make sure that the majority do not need complicated last-minute assembly or to be served immediately upon being cooked. Then consider your choice for combined colours, shapes, textures and flavours. Check that you have the appropriate pastry cutters and pastry cases, cocktail sticks and any other equipment needed for the recipes of your choice. Do as much as possible well in advance. Bread and pastry cases can be baked and stored in airtight tins the day before. Herbs used for garnishes can be chopped several hours before use, cling-filmed and stored in the refrigerator until needed. Thus with enough preplanning and preparation, there is no need for a hot and flustered host or hostess. Cool and confident, you may greet your guests in the knowledge that your cocktail party will be a success and, hopefully even for you, a pleasurable experience.

Fish & Shellfish

You will be simply spoilt for choice
with this delicious catch of fishy
treats

(All recipes make or serve 24)

Fish fresh, smoked and pickled, different fish roes and several types of shellfish provide a wide and varied choice of tasty and attractive fillings and toppings for canapés. Some are influenced by Scandinavia, originating from the smörgasbord. Gravlax – pickled salmon heady with the scent of dill – is one example; anchovy-flavoured appetisers with beetroot or tiny cubed potato are others. Mediterranean influences are here too in the form of squid and olive brochettes, mozzarella batons wrapped in salmon, and fragrant leaves of basil that envelope smoked mussels.

Translucent eggs of salmon roe form a particularly pretty addition to the smoked eel canapé. Black and red lumpfish roe adorn others. For pure visual enchantment however, the tiny silver-skinned whitebait, snugly fitted into bread barquettes, are irresistible.

KING PRAWNS WRAPPED IN CUCUMBER

12 king prawns in their
shells, peeled with
tail sections left on
8 tbsp olive oil
3 tbsp lemon juice
seasoning
3 cucumbers
dill sprigs

Blend 6 tbsp olive oil with lemon juice and seasoning. Pour over prawns and leave to absorb flavours for at least ½ hour.

Meanwhile, using a potato peeler, peel 2 cucumbers. Discard skins. Then cut thin strips from outer surfaces, sprinkle strips with salt and leave to soften. Cut remaining cucumber on the slant into 24 slices.

Drain prawns. Heat remaining oil and stir-fry until pink and cooked. Cool, then halve lengthwise with small, sharp scissors.

Rinse cucumber strips in cold water. Pat dry and wrap one round each halved prawn. Place onto cucumber slices and garnish with dill. Cling film and refrigerate.

GRAVLAX ON PUMPERNICKEL

*2lb (900g) fresh middle
  cut salmon*

*MARINADE
1 tbsp white
  peppercorns
1½–2oz (40–50g)
  salt
1½–2oz (40–50g)
  sugar
several bunches dill,
  finely chopped*

*FOR SERVING
6 large slices
  pumpernickel
1½–2oz (40–50g)
  butter
mustard and cress*

Scale salmon, remove centre bone and divide into 2 fillets. Dry on kitchen paper and remove any bones with tweezers. Crush peppercorns in a pestle and mortar, and mix with salt and sugar.

Sprinkle a layer of salt/sugar onto base of a gratin dish large enough to hold fish. Add a layer of dill. Place a fillet in dish, flesh side uppermost. Sprinkle half remaining salt/sugar mixture over fish, then half of dill. Place second fillet on top, skin side uppermost. Cover with remaining salt/sugar and dill.

Cling film and refrigerate for 2 days, turning fish over a couple of times. To serve, scrape spices off fish and cut it on the slant into thin slices.

For the croutes, cut crusts off pumpernickel slices and cut each into 4 equal pieces. Spread lightly with butter and cover with mustard and cress, and top with slices of gravlax. (Note: this recipe makes a large quantity and can be stored until needed.)

KIPPER AND SESAME FINGERS

6oz (175g) canned
  kipper fillets
juice and grated rind
  1 lemon
10oz (275g) puff pastry
1 egg, beaten
4 tbsp white sesame
  seeds
a little cayenne

Place kipper in a shallow bowl. Pour over lemon juice and sprinkle with rind. Leave to absorb the flavours for at least ½ hour.

Roll out puff pastry on a floured board and cut into thin pieces about 2½ × 1¼" (6×3cm) long. Drain kipper and cut into 24 narrow pieces. Place one on each piece of puff pastry. Brush top with egg, sprinkle with sesame seeds and a slight dusting of cayenne.

Bake in a preheated 220°C (425°F) Gas 7 oven for 15 minutes. Serve while still warm.

SQUID AND OLIVE BROCHETTES

1½–1¾lb (700–800g) squid
4 cloves garlic, crushed
3floz (75ml) olive oil
juice 2 limes
sprig rosemary, crushed
seasoning
4 slices wheatmeal bread, ½" (1cm) thick
12 large black olives, halved and stoned

Clean squid by pulling off heads. Cut tentacles off head and reserve. Remove and discard hard cartilage and any other remains inside squid. Remove purple membranes from outside of squid. Wash well and dry on kitchen paper. Cut squid bodies into long strips and separate tentacles.

Place squid in a bowl with garlic, 1floz (25ml) olive oil, lime juice, rosemary and seasoning, and leave to marinate for 2 hours.

Cut bread into 24 × ½" (1cm) cubes. When squid is marinated, heat a little olive oil in a frying pan and brown the bread cubes quickly all over. Remove from pan. Add a little more oil, and heat and fry squid, turning it all the time until cooked through, about 3–4 minutes. Drain on kitchen paper.

Place bread cubes on cocktail sticks, then thread fried squid onto sticks. Finish each cocktail stick with ½ black olive. Serve as soon as possible.

WHITEBAIT IN BREAD BARQUETTES

12 thin large slices
  white bread
melted butter for
  brushing
5oz (150g) whitebait
2 tbsp plain flour

generous pinch cayenne
pinch salt
oil for deep-frying
4–5floz (100–150ml)
  mayonnaise
mustard and cress

Cut each bread slice in half. Push bread into small barquette cases, and trim edges with scissors. Brush with melted butter and bake in a preheated 220°C (425°F) Gas 7 oven until golden brown, about 10 minutes. Leave to cool.

Meanwhile, wipe whitebait on kitchen paper, discarding any damaged fish. Mix flour with cayenne and salt. Dust flour mixture over fish, making sure it is evenly coated. Heat oil in a pan (it is hot enough when a stale bread cube browns in 1 minute). Fry whitebait, in small batches, for about 2 minutes. Move them gently just after immersion in the oil to prevent sticking together. Drain on kitchen paper and allow to cool a little.

Meanwhile, divide mayonnaise between barquettes. Place 2–4 fishes in each one, according to size. Top with a few strands of mustard and cress.

SMOKED COD CROQUETTES

FILLING
*1 lb (450g) smoked cod
    fillet*
1 oz (25g) butter
1 oz (25g) plain flour
1/2 pt (300ml) milk
2 tbsp grated parmesan
*2 tbsp finely chopped
    parsley*
seasoning

COATING
8 tbsp plain flour
1 egg, beaten
*3 tbsp dried
    breadcrumbs*
1/2 tsp cayenne
oil for deep-frying
paprika for dusting

Poach cod in water until just cooked, a
few minutes. Drain well and remove skin.
Flake and set aside.

Melt butter in a pan. Add flour and cook
over low heat for a couple of minutes,
stirring all the time. Remove from heat. Heat
milk until almost boiling and stir gradually
into the pan. Return to heat and cook for a
couple of minutes. Remove from heat and
add fish, parmesan and parsley. Season.

Spoon mixture into a shallow dish and
leave until cold. Cut into 24 equal pieces.
Mould pieces with lightly floured hands into
cylinder shapes.

Spread 6 tbsp flour onto a flat surface.
Roll cylinders in the flour and then dip into
beaten egg. Mix remaining flour with
breadcrumbs and cayenne. Spread onto a flat
surface and coat the egg-dipped croquettes
in the mixture. Refrigerate for 15 minutes.

Heat oil in a deep-fryer. Cook croquettes
until golden brown, drain on kitchen paper
and dust with paprika. Serve hot or cold.

SUSAN'S MONKFISH AIGRETTES

3oz (75g) fresh
   monkfish fillet, cut
   into 24 cubes

MARINADE
1 tbsp soy sauce
1 tbsp lemon juice
black pepper
small clove garlic,
   crushed

CHOUX PASTRY
2oz (50g) butter
1/4pt (150ml) water
2 1/2oz (65g) plain flour,
   sifted
2 eggs, lightly beaten
oil for deep-frying

Mix marinade ingredients and pour over fish cubes. Leave for about ½ hour, turning once in a while. Drain well.

Place butter and water in a saucepan. Heat gently until butter is melted, then bring to boil. Remove from heat and add all flour at once, beating mixture with a wooden spoon. Return to heat and continue beating until mixture forms a ball, leaving the sides of the pan. Allow to cool a little. Add eggs, a little at a time, beating vigorously all the time.

Heat oil in a deep-fryer. Use two teapoons to help you wrap up pieces of fish in pastry. Place a monkfish piece in one spoon, pick up enough pastry to cover fish cube with the other spoon, and roll the two together to a form a rough ball. Deep-fry until golden and rise to surface. Drain on kitchen paper and serve as soon as possible.

SALMON AND DILL CRACKERS

*9oz (250g) fresh
    salmon fillet, skinned
juice 1 lemon
bunch dill, finely
    chopped*

*seasoning
4 sheets filo pastry,
    12×8" (30×20cm)
oil for brushing*

Cut salmon into strips 1½" (4cm) long and ¾" (2cm) wide. Remove any bones with tweezers. Place strips in a shallow dish, and sprinkle with juice, dill and seasoning.

Work with 1 sheet of pastry at a time to prevent drying out. Brush uppermost surface with oil, then fold sheet in half to form a 6×8" (15×20cm) rectangle. Again brush surface with oil. Slice pastry into 6 equal pieces (halve lengthwise and cut across into thirds).

Place a salmon strip on centre of pastry piece, along one edge. Roll pastry up round fish. Twist ends to form a cracker shape, and brush surface with oil. Repeat with remaining pastry and salmon.

Bake in a preheated 200°C (400°F) Gas 6 oven for 10 minutes or until golden brown. Serve while still warm.

The crackers can be prepared, filled and frozen, and baked straight from freezer when needed.

SMOKED TROUT PASTRIES

PASTRY
6oz (175g) puff pastry
½ egg, beaten
black onion seeds (from
    Indian grocers)

FILLING
3oz (75g) ready-made
    trout pâté
grated rind ½ lemon
black pepper

Roll out pastry very thinly on a floured board and cut into 24 squares, approx. 2½″ (6cm).

Blend together pâté and lemon rind. Season with black pepper. Divide filling between pastry squares, spooning onto one half to leave edges clear. Brush edges with water. Fold pastry over filling to form triangles and push edges firmly together with a fork.

Place pastries on a dampened baking sheet. Brush tops with beaten egg and sprinkle with black onion seeds. Bake in a preheated 200°C (400°F) Gas 6 oven for 10 minutes or until golden brown. Serve while still warm, or reheat before serving.

SMOKED EEL MORSELS ON BLACK BREAD

24 slices soft black rye
  bread
1–1½oz (25–40g) soft
  butter
2 tbsp hot horseradish
  relish
8oz (225g) smoked eel
  fillet, skinned
3oz (75g) pickled dill
  cucumbers
4 tbsp salmon or
  lumpfish roe

Remove crusts from bread, spread thinly with butter then cut into 24×1½" (4cm) squares. Spread horseradish relish over bread. Cut eel fillet on the slant into 1" (2.5cm) pieces. Slice cucumbers thinly.

Arrange eel fillet and cucumber on bread squares. Top with a little salmon or lumpfish roe. Cling film and store in a cool place until ready to serve.

SMOKED SALMON AND MOZZARELLA BATONS

6oz (175g) mozzarella
5–6oz (150–175g)
thinly sliced smoked
salmon
bunch dill, finely
chopped
crushed black
peppercorns

Slice cheese into strips ½″ (1cm) wide and 1½″ (4cm) long. Slice salmon into strips the same length as cheese but a fraction wider. Wrap each baton of cheese in a strip of smoked salmon. Dip one end in dill and the other in peppercorns. Cling film and store in a cool place until serving.

ANCHOVY AND BEETROOT APPETISERS

6 anchovy fillets
4floz (100ml) milk
4 cooked beetroot,
    diced small
1 small red onion, diced
    small
1 gherkin, diced small
½ dessert apple, diced

1 tbsp capers, finely
    chopped
seasoning
24 slices soft black rye
    bread
4–5 tbsp mayonnaise
mustard and cress

S oak anchovy fillets in milk for about ½
hour. Drain anchovies, dry well on
kitchen paper and cut into tiny dice. Mix all
diced and chopped ingredients, and season.

Remove crusts and cut out 24 squares
from bread slices, about 1½–2" (4–5cm).
Spread mayonnaise onto bread. Cut little
bunches of mustard and cress and place a
bunch on each piece of bread. Pile anchovy/
beetroot mixture onto bread squares, cling
film and keep in a cool place until serving.

GARLIC-SCENTED OYSTERS EN CROUTE

24 slices white bread,
  ¾" (2cm) thick
6oz (175g) soft butter
grated rind ½ lemon

1 clove garlic, crushed
24 oysters
black pepper
dill sprigs

Remove bread crusts and, using a small pastry cutter, cut out 24 rounds (or ovals if preferred). Make a hollow in centre of bread large enough to hold an oyster. Melt 2oz (50g) of butter and stir in lemon rind. Brush prepared bread with butter mixture.

Blend remaining butter with garlic. Open oysters and remove carefully from shells. Slip an oyster into each hollow. Top with little knobs of garlic butter and sprinkle with black pepper. Place on a baking sheet and cook in a preheated 220°C (425°F) Gas 7 oven for 10–12 minutes. Serve while still warm, garnished with sprigs of dill.

MUSSEL AND PRAWN KEBABS

24 large fresh mussels
48 firm peeled, cooked prawns
juice 1 lime
2 tbsp olive oil, plus extra for grilling
seasoning
lime zest

Discard any mussels with broken shells or which do not close when tapped sharply with the back of a knife. Wash mussels well. Place in a saucepan with a little water to not quite cover and bring slowly to boil. Simmer gently for a couple of minutes until all mussels have opened. Any which remain closed must be discarded. Leave to cool and remove carefully from shells.

Place mussels and prawns in a shallow bowl. Blend together lime juice and olive oil and pour over shellfish. Sprinkle with a little salt and plenty of freshly ground black pepper. Leave to absorb flavours for at least ½ hour.

Thread mussels and prawns onto tiny skewers – prawn, mussel, prawn on each one. Brush with a little olive oil and grill under a hot grill for a couple of minutes. Garnish with lime zest and serve hot.

ITALIAN ANGELS ON HORSEBACK

24 oysters
2 tbsp lemon juice
black pepper
4–5oz (100–150g)
   sliced parma ham
4oz (100g) butter
24 slices white bread
chopped chives for
   dipping
lemon zest

Open oysters and remove carefully from shells. Sprinkle with lemon juice and freshly ground black pepper. Cut parma ham into thin strips. Wrap each oyster in a strip of ham, securing with a cocktail stick.

Heat 3oz (75g) of butter in a frying pan. Cook angels for about 2–3 minutes, turning over a couple of times.

Remove crusts and cut bread into 24×1½″ (4cm) squares. Spread with remaining butter. Dip edges of bread in chopped chives.

Place an angel on top of each bread square. Garnish with lemon zest and serve as soon as possible.

MUSSELS ON MOCK SEAWEED

6oz (175g) shortcrust
   pastry
24 fresh mussels

MARINADE
2 tbsp lemon juice
1 tbsp sweet sherry
2 tsp dark soy sauce
2 tsp sesame oil
1 small clove garlic,
   crushed
$\frac{1}{2}$ tsp grated root
   ginger

MOCK SEAWEED
6–7oz (175–200g)
   curly endive
oil for deep-frying

Line 24 small pastry cases (shell-shaped ones if you can get them) with thinly rolled out pastry. Bake in a preheated 180°C (350°F) Gas 4 oven for 6–8 minutes. Leave to cool before removing from tins.

Discard any mussels with broken shells or which do not close when tapped sharply with the back of a knife. Wash mussels well. Place in a saucepan with a little water to not quite cover and bring slowly to boil. Simmer gently for a couple of minutes until all mussels have opened. Any which remain closed must be discarded. Leave to cool and remove carefully from shells.

Mix together all ingredients for marinade and pour over mussels. Leave to absorb flavours for an hour or so, gently turning mussels once in a while.

Meanwhile, shred curly endive very finely. Heat oil in a pan. (It is hot enough when a stale bread cube browns in 1 minute.) Plunge shredded endive into hot oil. When dark green, translucent and crisp, it is ready. Do not let it brown. Drain endive well on kitchen paper.

Drain marinade from mussels. Line pastry cases with 'seaweed'. Place a mussel in the centre of each case and serve.

ANCHOVY AND POTATO EN CROUTE

*24 thin slices brown
  bread*
*melted butter for
  brushing*
18 anchovy fillets
½pt (300ml) milk
4 tbsp cooking oil
1 onion, finely chopped
*8oz (225g) cooked
  potato, diced small*
*1 heaped tbsp capers,
  chopped*
pinch allspice
seasoning
finely chopped chives
*tiny anchovy slivers
  (optional)*

Push bread into 24 small, shallow round
pastry cases. Trim edges with scissors.
Brush with melted butter and bake in a
preheated 220°C (425°F) Gas 7 oven until
golden brown, about 10 minutes. Leave
to cool.

Meanwhile, soak anchovies in milk for 10
minutes. Heat oil in a frying pan and cook
onion over medium heat until golden.
Remove onion from pan. Add diced potato
and fry until golden, stirring frequently.
Remove from heat and mix with onion.

Drain the anchovies, rinse quickly in cold
water and dry well on kitchen paper. Cut
into very fine dice and stir into potato
mixture. Add capers, allspice and seasoning.
Pile mixture into bread cases and sprinkle
with chives. Serve hot or cold, garnished
with anchovy slivers if liked.

30

COD'S ROE AND CRAB MEAT PATTIES

4oz (100g) cooked
   cod's roe
4oz (100g) cooked
   white crab meat
2oz (50g) cream
   cheese
1 egg yolk
grated rind 1 lemon
1 tbsp finely chopped
   parsley
1oz (25g) fresh
   breadcrumbs
seasoning
oil for frying
1 cucumber
2–3 tbsp soured cream
small dill sprigs

Blend together cod's roe, crab meat, cream cheese and egg yolk. Stir in lemon rind, parsley and breadcrumbs. Mix well, and season.

Shape mixture into tiny patties. Heat oil in a non-stick frying pan and brown patties until crisp and golden, turning once. Leave to cool.

Cut 24×¼″ (0.5cm) thick slices from cucumber. Place a fish patty on each one. Top with a little soured cream and garnish with sprigs of dill. Cling film and store in a cool place until serving.

SHRIMP AND BANANA WITH COCONUT TOP

24 slices white bread
3 tbsp cooking oil
2½oz (65g) creamed
   coconut
2½ tsp hot curry
   powder
3floz (75ml) lemon
   juice
2 bananas, diced
8oz (225g) peeled,
   cooked shrimps
3floz (75ml)
   mayonnaise
2 tbsp desiccated
   coconut
mustard and cress

Line 24 small barquette pastry cases with
bread. Trim edges with scissors. Brush
with oil and bake in a preheated 220°C
(425°F) Gas 7 oven for 10 minutes. Cool.

Melt creamed coconut over very low
heat. Add curry powder, lemon juice and
bananas. Cook very gently for a minute or so,
stirring all the time. Remove from heat.
Reserving 24 shrimps for garnish, stir into
mixture with mayonnaise.

Spoon filling into bread cases. Heat a
frying pan and roast coconut until golden,
stirring all the time. Scatter over top of
filling. Garnish with shrimps and mustard
and cress. Serve as soon as possible.

CLAM AND TOMATO TARTLETS

24 slices white bread
cooking oil for brushing
1 lb (450g) tomatoes
8oz (225g) shelled,
cooked clams
1 clove garlic, crushed
black pepper
3 tbsp mayonnaise
3 tbsp chopped
coriander
coriander leaves for
garnish

Line 24 small tartlet tins with bread slices and trim edges with scissors. Brush with a little oil and bake in a preheated 220°C (425°F) Gas 7 oven until crisp and golden, about 10 minutes. Leave to cool.

Skin tomatoes by plunging briefly into boiling water one at a time. Quarter them, remove seeds and dice finely. Add clams and garlic. Season with black pepper. Set aside until just before serving.

Drain away any liquid and stir in mayonnaise and coriander. Fill tartlets with clam mixture, garnish with coriander and serve.

OCTOPUS AND WATERCRESS EN CROUTE

*FOR COOKING
   OCTOPUS*
*2lb (900g) octopus
   tentacles*
½ lemon
2 bayleaves
10 black peppercorns
salt

FILLING
*½ red onion, finely
   chopped*
3floz (75ml) olive oil
*3floz (75ml) red wine
   vinegar*
2 cloves garlic, crushed
*1 tbsp chopped
   tarragon*
seasoning

FOR SERVING
24 slices white bread
3 tbsp cooking oil
4 tbsp mayonnaise
bunch watercress
red onion rings

Wash octopus. Place in a saucepan with lemon, bayleaves, peppercorns, a little salt and enough water to cover. Bring to boil then simmer gently until octopus is tender, about 45 minutes, Leave to cool in the water. Then transfer octopus to a shallow bowl.

Scatter onion over octopus, retaining a little for garnish. Blend oil, vinegar, garlic and tarragon and pour over octopus. Season well. Cling film and refrigerate overnight.

Line 24 small pastry cases with bread slices and trim edges with scissors. Brush with oil and bake in a preheated 220°C (425°F) Gas 7 oven for 10 minutes. Leave to cool.

Divide mayonnaise between bread cases. Line cases with watercress leaves. Slice octopus tentacles and arrange in lined bread cases. Garnish with onion rings. Cling film and store in a cool place until serving.

SMOKED MUSSELS IN BASIL LEAVES

24 large basil leaves
24 canned smoked
  mussels, approx.
  3.6oz (105g) can

1 tbsp olive oil
2 tsp lemon juice
2 tbsp water
3 tomatoes

Wash basil leaves and remove coarse
stalks. Dry on kitchen paper and lay
out flat. Place a smoked mussel in centre of
each leaf. Fold over edges and form into neat
parcels. Place parcels in a frying pan. Add
olive oil, lemon juice and water and bring to
boil. Turn down heat and simmer very gently
until basil leaves are just soft, a couple of
minutes. Remove from heat and set aside.

Halve tomatoes, discard seeds, and cut
into 48 slivers.

Thread a tomato sliver onto a cocktail
stick. Thread mussel parcel into cavity of
tomato sliver. Finish with another sliver of
tomato, skin side uppermost. Cling film and
store in a cool place until serving.

LUMPFISH ROE AND HALIBUT EN CROUTE

24 slices wheatmeal
    bread
3 tbsp cooking oil
4 tbsp mayonnaise
6oz (175g) red
    lumpfish roe

6 slices smoked halibut
    (from quality
    delicatessens) or
    smoked salmon,
    about 8oz (225g)
dill or chervil sprigs

Push bread into 24 small pastry cases
(square ones are particularly pretty).
Trim edges with scissors. Brush with oil and
bake in a preheated 220°C (425°F) Gas 7
oven for 10 minutes. Leave to cool.

When cold, spoon a little mayonnaise
into each bread case. Divide lumpfish roe
between bread cases. Cut each halibut
slice into 4 long, narrow strips. Starting at
narrowest end of each strip, roll it up. When
about ¾ of slice is rolled up, curl remainder
of strip loosely to give a rose-shaped effect.
Place a rolled-up fish in centre of each bread
case. Garnish with sprigs of dill or chervil.
Cling film and store in a cool place until
serving.

PRAWN AND SESAME TRIANGLES

3oz (75g) curd cheese
1 egg yolk
8oz (225g) peeled,
 cooked prawns,
 roughly chopped
1 spring onion, finely
 chopped
1 tsp grated lemon rind
pinch cayenne
seasoning
6 slices white bread
2 eggs
1 tbsp single cream
2 tbsp white sesame
 seeds

B lend curd cheese and egg yolk. Stir in prawns, spring onion and lemon rind. Season with cayenne and black pepper and a little salt if necessary. Set aside.

Remove crusts from bread slices. Beat eggs with cream and season. Dip slices of bread, both sides, in egg mixture. Place bread on a greased baking sheet.

Spread prawn mixture on top of bread slices, scatter with sesame seeds and bake in a preheated 200°C (400°F) Gas 6 oven for 20 minutes. Cool a little then cut each slice into 4 triangular pieces. Serve while still warm.

SOFT ROE ON A BED OF SORREL

24 slices white bread
3 tbsp cooking oil
12oz (350g) soft roe
3 tbsp plain flour
grated rind ½ lemon
pinch cayenne
seasoning
3oz (75g) butter
2 tbsp water
6oz (175g) sorrel or
 small spinach leaves,
 washed and trimmed
cayenne for dusting

Line 24 small pastry cases with bread slices. Trim edges with scissors, brush lightly with oil and bake in a preheated 220°C (425°F) Gas 7 oven for 10 minutes. Cool.

Wash roe and dry thoroughly on kitchen paper. Mix flour with lemon rind, cayenne, and seasoning. Coat roe with flour mixture. Heat 2oz (50g) of butter in a non-stick frying pan. Cook roes, a few at a time, over medium heat until golden brown. Drain well on kitchen paper.

Heat remaining butter and water in a small pan. Add sorrel or spinach leaves and cook until just tender. Drain well.

Line bread cases with sorrel or spinach leaves. Top with soft roe and dust with cayenne. Serve as soon as possible.

FINGERS WITH FISH PÂTÉ AND ROE

8 slices wheatmeal
   bread
2 tbsp cooking oil
4oz (100g) smooth fish
   pâté, e.g. buckling
   pâté
2 hard-boiled egg yolks,
   chopped
2oz (50g) salmon roe,
   plus red and black
   lumpfish roe
mustard and cress for
   garnish

Remove crusts from bread, forming nice straight edges. Brush surfaces lightly with oil and place on a baking sheet. Bake in a preheated 220°C (425°F) Gas 7 oven for 10 minutes. Leave to cool.

Spread fish pâté over ⅔ of each bread croute. Cover the remaining area with stripes of chopped egg yolks and different coloured roes.

Cut each bread piece into 3 fingers. Garnish pâté part of fingers with mustard and cress. Cling film and store in a cool place until serving.

TROUT WITH MAYONNAISE AND CAPERS

8oz (225g) fresh trout
    fillet
2 slices lemon
6 black peppercorns
salt
24 slices wheatmeal
    bread
3 tbsp oil
4 tbsp mayonnaise
2 tbsp green
    peppercorn mustard
2 tsp capers, chopped
1oz (25g) flaked
    almonds, toasted
small chives

Place trout in a shallow pan. Add
lemon slices, peppercorns and a little
salt. Add enough water to barely cover fish
and poach gently until just cooked, a couple
of minutes. Leave to cool. Remove skin and
flake fish, removing any bones, and set aside.

Remove crusts and cut bread into 24
2½×1½″ (6×4cm) rectangles. Place on a
baking sheet, brush with oil and bake in a
preheated 220°C (425°F) Gas 7 oven for 10
minutes. Leave to cool.

Blend together mayonnaise, mustard and
capers. Spread over bread croutes, reserving
a little for top. Arrange flaked trout on top of
croutes. Top with remaining mayonnaise and
garnish with almonds and chives.

Poultry & Game

Take your pick of a delectable variety
of chicken, duck and turkey bites

(All recipes make or serve 24)

Poultry lends itself to being cooked and flavoured in a multitude of ways. Sold conveniently in fillets, chicken, duck and turkey breasts provide a particularly useful basis for a tasty range of canapés. Included here is pistachio-stuffed chicken, duck marinated and cooked in red wine and walnut oil, topped with pickled kumquats, and turkey escalopes rolled round slices of salami and dolcelatte cheese.

Chicken livers combine with walnuts in a pastry wrapping or are served in kebabs, spiced with juniper. Duck livers feature in a mousse, filling tiny pastry horns. And slivers of smoked duck and chicken make succulent and pretty party pieces in no time at all.

SMOKED CHICKEN WITH GRAPES

*12 thin slices white
 bread*
6 tbsp cooking oil
*7–8oz (200–225g)
 smoked chicken
 breast fillet, cut into
 thin strips*
*24 grapes, seeded and
 cut into thin strips*
4 tbsp mayonnaise
*6 radicchio leaves, torn
 into pieces*
mustard and cress

Remove bread crusts and flatten slices
using a rolling pin. Cut each into 2
triangles. Brush with oil on both sides. Form
bread triangles into cone shapes, place on a
baking sheet, joins downwards, and brown in
a preheated 220°C (425°F) Gas 7 oven for 10
minutes. Leave to cool.

Place chicken and grapes in a bowl. Stir
in mayonnaise. Arrange radicchio and
chicken mixture in cones and garnish with
mustard and cress. Cling film and refrigerate
until serving.

SPICED CHICKEN WINGS

12 chicken wings

MARINADE
2 tbsp soy sauce
2 tbsp pineapple juice
juice 1/2 lemon
1 tbsp sesame oil
1 tbsp Szechwan
  peppercorns, crushed
1 tbsp harisa paste or
  chilli sauce
1 clove garlic, crushed
salt

Trim off bony ends of chicken wings. Remove any feathers with tweezers. Divide wings in two along joint.

Blend together all marinade ingredients. Place chicken wing halves in a shallow dish. Pour over marinade and leave to absorb flavours for about 1 hour, turning pieces once in a while.

Grill chicken under a medium heat until brown and crisp, brushing with a little marinade every so often. Serve hot or cold. If serving cold, cling film and store in a cool place until needed.

46

CHICKEN LIVER KEBABS WITH JUNIPER

10oz (275g) chicken livers
14oz (400g) streaky bacon, approx. 12 rashers
24 sage leaves
10 juniper berries, crushed
black pepper
24 seedless grapes

Wash chicken livers well and dry on kitchen paper. Cut into 24 pieces and set aside.

Half bacon lengthwise into 24 strips. Lay flat on a board. Place a sage leaf on each bacon strip, then sprinkle with crushed juniper and black pepper. Place chicken liver piece in the centre of each bacon slice. The liver should protrude a little at either end of the bacon. Roll bacon round liver and secure with a cocktail stick.

Bake in a preheated 220°C (425°F) Gas 7 oven for 15 minutes, turning livers half-way through cooking period.

Leave to cool a little, then transfer to clean cocktail sticks and push a grape on the end of each. Equally delicious hot or cold.

CHICKEN PIECES WITH SPICY PEANUT DIP

14oz (400g) skinned
  chicken breast fillet
2–3 tbsp cooking oil
12 × 1/4" (0.5cm) slices
  cucumber, halved

MARINADE
4 tbsp soy sauce
2 tbsp lemon juice
seasoning

SAUCE
3 tbsp smooth peanut
  butter
2 cloves garlic, crushed
2 tsp harisa paste or
  chilli sauce
5 tbsp lemon juice

Cut chicken into 24×1″ (2.5cm) cubes.
Place in a bowl. Mix soy sauce with
lemon juice and pour over chicken. Season
and leave to absorb flavours for at least ½
hour.

Drain chicken. Heat oil in a frying pan.
Brown chicken until nice and golden. Turn
down heat and cook for a little longer until
cooked right through. Set aside while
making sauce.

Warm peanut butter very gently until
soft. Add garlic, harisa paste and lemon
juice. Blend well. Add enough hot water to
make sauce of dipping consistency.

Thread a cucumber piece and a chicken
cube onto each cocktail stick. Pour sauce
into a shallow dish and surround with the
chicken sticks.

Serve sauce still warm as it tends to
thicken when cold. (Reheat gently if
necessary before serving.)

CHICKEN IN SPINACH WRAPPING

14oz (400g) skinned
  chicken breast fillet
3 tbsp olive oil
4 tbsp dry white wine
2 tbsp chopped
  tarragon

seasoning
24 undamaged, large
  lettuce leaves
8 slices parma ham, cut
  into long thin strips

Cut chicken into 24 bite-size pieces. Place in a shallow bowl. Blend together oil, wine, tarragon and seasoning. Pour this marinade over chicken and leave to absorb flavours for at least 1 hour. Then transfer to a shallow pan and poach chicken until cooked through, 5–6 minutes. Leave to cool.

Meanwhile, wash lettuce well and plunge one at a time into boiling water just long enough to make them go limp, a couple of seconds only. Refresh in cold water and pat dry on kitchen paper.

Drain chicken. Place a piece of chicken in centre of each lettuce leaf. Fold over edges to form neat parcels. Wrap a strip of parma ham around each parcel and tie parcel-fashion. Cling film and refrigerate until ready to serve.

CHICKEN AND MUSHROOM ROULADES

8 skinned, boned
  chicken thighs
4 tbsp olive oil
4oz (100g) open
  mushrooms, roughly
  chopped
8 black olives, chopped
1oz (25g) fresh, brown
  breadcrumbs
1 small clove garlic,
  crushed

½ tbsp chopped
  tarragon
seasoning
24 slices wheatmeal
  bread
4–5 tbsp mayonnaise
4–5 tbsp finely
  chopped chives

Place chicken between sheets of cling film and flatten by beating with a rolling pin. Heat half olive oil in a pan. Add mushrooms and cook gently until soft. Place in a food processor with olives and breadcrumbs and process until fairly smooth. Add garlic and tarragon. Season.

Spread mushroom mixture over chicken. Roll up and secure with cocktail sticks and fine string. Place on a foil-lined roasting tray. Brush with remaining olive oil and season. Cook in a preheated 170°C (325°F) Gas 3 oven for 25 minutes. Leave to cool before slicing the chicken thinly on the slant.

Remove crusts and cut bread into 1½×2½" (4×6cm) rectangles. Spread with mayonnaise, and scatter on chives. Divide chicken roulades over bread.

LEMON CHICKEN AND AVOCADO EN CROUTE

*FOR COOKING
   CHICKEN*
*10oz (275g) skinned
   chicken breast fillet*
grated rind 1 lemon
juice ½ lemon
2 tbsp olive oil
seasoning

FOR SERVING
24 slices white bread
3 tbsp olive oil
6 tbsp mayonnaise
3 tbsp Greek yogurt
*1 tbsp chopped
   tarragon*
*1 ripe avocado, cut into
   triangular pieces*
lemon juice
*5 – 6 radicchio leaves,
   very finely shredded*
lemon zest

Line a roasting tray with foil. Place chicken on foil and sprinkle with lemon rind, juice and olive oil. Season. Cook in a preheated 180°C (350°F) Gas 4 oven for 20 minutes, turning chicken once in a while. Cool completely.

Push bread into 24 small round or oval pastry cases. Trim edges with scissors. Brush with olive oil and bake in a preheated 220°C (425°F) Gas 7 oven for 10 minutes. Leave to cool.

Meanwhile, blend together mayonnaise, yogurt and tarragon. When bread croutes are cold, spread mayonnaise mixture over them.

Slice chicken across thinly. Arrange with avocado pieces on bread. Brush a little lemon juice over avocado to stop discolouration. Top with radicchio and lemon zest to garnish.

Cool and refrigerate until ready to serve – do not prepare too far in advance as avocado will discolour after some time.

CHICKEN IN RICE PAPER

6oz (175g) skinned
  chicken breast fillet
24 galettes de riz
  (triangular sheets of
  rice paper, from
  Chinese
  supermarkets)

MARINADE
2 tbsp soy sauce
2 tbsp lemon juice
1 tsp sesame oil

FILLING
1 red pepper, cut into
  thin strips
2 spring onions, cut into
  thin strips
2 eggs, beaten
oil for deep-frying

Cut chicken into thin strips. Place in a bowl. Mix together soy sauce, lemon juice and sesame oil. Pour over chicken and leave for at least ½ hour. Drain well.

Soak *galettes de riz* in cold water, a few at a time, for 10 minutes to make them soft and pliable. Pile on top of each other, separated by sheets of cling film. Dry each *galette* with kitchen paper as you use it.

Place a *galette* on a flat surface, and place some chicken strips in the centre. Top with pepper and spring onion. Brush edges with egg and roll up, folding in edges. Brush with egg to seal. Repeat with other galettes.

Heat oil in a deep-fryer and cook rolls until crisp and golden, turning them over once in a while to brown evenly. Drain off excess fat on kitchen paper. Serve warm.

CHICKEN LIVER AND WALNUT ENVELOPES

FILLING
8oz (225g) chicken
   livers
1oz (25g) butter
2 tbsp finely chopped
   onion
1oz (25g) walnuts,
   chopped
pinch thyme
seasoning
1 tbsp single cream
1 tbsp dry sherry

PASTRY
12oz (350g) puff pastry
1 egg, beaten
1 tbsp milk
2 tbsp poppy seeds

Wash chicken livers well and dry on kitchen paper. Cut into small dice. Heat butter in a heavy pan and brown livers quickly. Add onion and walnuts and cook until onion is soft and translucent. Add thyme and seasoning. Stir in cream and sherry. Leave until cold.

Roll out puff pastry thinly on a floured surface. Cut out 24×3″ (7.5cm) squares. Place a little filling in centre of each. Blend beaten egg with milk and brush edges. Fold corners in to form small envelopes. Pinch edges together tightly. Refrigerate for at least ½ hour.

Brush pastries with egg wash, sprinkle with poppy seeds and bake in a preheated 200°C (400°F) Gas 6 oven for 15 minutes. Serve while still warm.

These pastries can be filled and frozen, then brushed with egg yolk, sprinkled with poppy seeds and baked just before using.

SAFFRON CHICKEN IN PUFF PASTRY

FILLING
pinch saffron strands
8floz (225ml) milk
½oz (15g) butter
2oz (50g) mushrooms,
  chopped
½oz (15g) plain flour
5oz (150g) cooked
  chicken, diced small
seasoning

PASTRY
12oz (350g) puff pastry
1 egg, beaten
1½–2oz (40–50g)
  flaked almonds

Place saffron in a small saucepan. Pour milk over and leave to stand for at least ½ hour. Melt butter in a pan. Add mushrooms and cook until soft and excess liquid evaporated. Stir in flour and continue to cook briefly. Remove from heat.

Heat milk with saffron to almost boiling point. Stir gradually into mushroom mixture. Return to heat and bring to boil. Simmer for a couple of minutes. Remove from heat and leave to cool. Add diced chicken and season well.

Roll out puff pastry thinly on a floured surface. Using a small pastry cutter, cut out 24 rounds. Place a scant teaspoon of filling on one half of each pastry round, leaving edges clear. Brush edges with beaten egg and fold pastry rounds in half, pinching edges together firmly.

Brush surfaces with beaten egg. Crush almonds gently between your fingers and scatter over pastry surfaces. Bake in a preheated 220°C (425°F) Gas 7 oven for 10–12 minutes. Serve while still warm or reheat before serving.

CHINESE CHICKEN BALLS

*12oz (350g) skinned
chicken breast fillet
3oz (75g) shiitake
mushrooms, very
finely chopped
8 small spring onions,
very finely chopped
3 tbsp chopped
coriander
4 tsp cornflour
large pinch chilli
1 tbsp soy sauce
beaten egg for binding
oil for frying
soy sauce for dipping*

Mince chicken and place in a bowl. Add all remaining ingredients, except egg, and mix well. Add just enough beaten egg to bind mixture. Roll into small balls.

Heat oil in a non-stick pan. Add chicken balls and fry until golden brown and cooked right through. Drain on kitchen paper and serve, preferably while still warm, on cocktail sticks with extra soy sauce in a small bowl for dipping.

PISTACHIO-STUFFED CHICKEN WITH TOMATO

12oz (350g) skinned
   chicken breast fillet
3oz (75g) soft butter
3oz (75g) pistachio
   nuts, coarsely
   chopped
large pinch coriander
   seasoning
3 tbsp olive oil
24 slices wheatmeal
   bread
approx. 18 cherry
   tomatoes, sliced
chervil sprigs

Place chicken between sheets of cling film and flatten by beating with a rolling pin. Spread half the butter thinly over the flattened chicken. Scatter nuts over surface. Sprinkle with coriander and seasoning. Roll up and secure with cocktail sticks. Brush surface with olive oil.

Cook in a preheated 180°C (350°F) Gas 4 oven for 25 minutes. Leave to cool. Remove cocktail sticks and slice stuffed chicken thinly.

Spread remaining butter over bread. Using a small pastry cutter, cut out 24 rectangles. Top with tomato slices and then with chicken slices. Garnish with chervil. Cling film and store in a cool place until serving.

CHICKEN AND WATERCRESS IN FILO PASTRY

FILLING
3oz (75g) watercress
5oz (150g) cooked
chicken, diced small
or minced
6 black olives, finely
chopped
1 clove garlic, crushed
2oz (50g) curd cheese
seasoning

PASTRY
4 sheets filo pastry,
8×2" (20×30cm)
5–6floz (150–175ml)
olive oil
2 tbsp white sesame
seeds

Cook watercress in a tiny amount of water until just soft. Drain and chop quite finely. Place in a bowl and mix in remaining ingredients. Season.

Working with one sheet of pastry at a time (keep others covered with cling film to prevent drying out), brush uppermost surface with oil. Fold sheet in half and brush with oil. Using scissors, cut sheet in half lengthwise.

Place a thin sausage of filling along length of one pastry strip. Roll lengthwise up into a thin sausage shape. Brush with oil all over. Cut across into 3 equal pieces and roll each up into coils. Brush with oil. Repeat with the other pastry strip. Continue with remaining 3 sheets.

Place pastry coils on an oiled baking tray and sprinkle with sesame seeds. Bake in a preheated 190°C (375°F) Gas 5 oven for 15 minutes. Serve while still warm or reheat before serving.

DUCK LIVER MOUSSE IN PASTRY HORNS

6oz (175g) puff pastry
a little flour for dusting
1 egg, beaten

FILLING
9oz (250g) smooth
    duck liver pâté
3 tbsp Greek yogurt
2 tbsp brandy
green peppercorns in
    brine

Roll out pastry thinly and cut into 24 strips, approx. 8" (20cm) long and ¾" (2cm) wide.

Dust 24 small pastry horn tins well with flour. Wrap a pastry strip round each horn tin, starting at the tip and allowing pastry to overlap by about ¼" (0.5cm). Brush generously with beaten egg. Arrange, join downwards, on dampened baking sheets and bake in a preheated 180°C (350°F) Gas 4 oven for 5 minutes or until golden brown. Cool slightly then remove carefully from tins by twisting horns lightly. Set aside to cool completely.

Blend together filling ingredients until smooth. Pipe into pastry horns and garnish each tip with a couple of green peppercorns. Cling film and refrigerate until serving.

GLAZED SMOKED DUCK AND PRUNES

8 large stoned prunes
7 floz (200ml) port or
    red table wine
24 thin slices white
    bread
walnut oil for brushing
12oz (350g) smoked
    duck breast
3 tbsp blackcurrant
    jelly
1 tbsp water
tarragon sprigs

Soak prunes in port or wine for about 1 hour. Meanwhile, push bread into 24 small pastry cases (any shape will do). Trim edges with scissors. Brush with a little walnut oil and bake in a preheated 220°C (425°F) Gas 7 oven until golden brown, about 10 minutes. Leave to cool.

Drain prunes and cut into thin slivers. Cut duck breast into thin slivers, removing skin if preferred. Arrange prunes and duck strips attractively in bread cases.

Melt blackcurrant jelly in a pan with water. Brush prunes and duck with jelly, and top each croute with sprigs of tarragon.

MARINATED DUCK WITH KUMQUATS

14–16oz (400–450g)
duck breast fillet

MARINADE
6floz (175ml) red wine
1 tbsp walnut oil
½ onion, thinly sliced
seasoning

FOR COOKING
KUMQUATS
12 kumquats, sliced
1 tbsp dark brown
sugar
4 whole cloves

FOR SERVING
24 slices wheatmeal
bread
3 tbsp cooking oil
mustard and cress

Place duck in a shallow dish. Blend
together wine and oil for marinade. Place
onion on top of duck fillet, season and pour
over wine mixture. Cover and leave overnight.

Meanwhile, place kumquats in a small
pan. Add enough water to just cover and
bring to boil. Simmer for a couple of minutes.
Add sugar and cloves. Simmer a little longer
until soft but still holding shape. Cool.

Drain duck and dry on kitchen paper.
Place, skin side up, in a roasting tray. Roast
in a preheated 220°C (425°F) Gas 7 oven for
20 minutes, turning pieces over once.

Line 24 small pastry cases with bread
slices and trim edges with scissors. Brush
with oil and bake in a preheated 220°C
(425°F) Gas 7 oven for 10 minutes. Cool.

Slice duck thinly across. Pile into bread
cases. Top with pickled kumquat slices and
mustard and cress. Serve as soon as possible.

TINY TURKEY SPRING ROLLS

24 spring roll wrappers
 (from Chinese
 supermarkets)
oil for deep-frying

FILLING
5oz (150g) skinned
 turkey breast fillet,
 diced small
1 tbsp finely chopped
 spring onion

1oz (25g) beansprouts,
 chopped
5 shiitake mushrooms,
 chopped (optional)
1" (2.5cm) piece root
 ginger, peeled and
 finely chopped
1 clove garlic, crushed
seasoning

Mix together all filling ingredients and
season. Divide filling between spring
roll wrappers. Brush edges well with water to
seal and form into small rolls.

Heat oil and deep-fry spring rolls until
crisp and golden. Drain on kitchen paper and
serve hot. Reheat later if necessary.

TURKEY BITES WITH CORIANDER DIP

12oz (350g) turkey
  escalopes
oil for deep-frying

MARINADE
juice 2 limes
1 tsp grated lime rind
seasoning

BATTER
4oz (100g) plain flour
1/2 tsp turmeric
1/2 tsp cumin
pinch cayenne

salt
1/2 egg, beaten
1/4pt (150ml) cold
  water

DIP
7floz (200ml) Greek
  yogurt
1 tbsp lemon juice
1 clove garlic, crushed
salt
4 tbsp chopped
  coriander

Cut turkey pieces into 24 portions. Place in a bowl. Pour over lime juice, rind and seasoning. Leave to absorb flavours for about 1/2 hour.

Meanwhile, prepare batter. Sieve together flour, spices and salt in a bowl. Add egg, beating with a wooden spoon, and gradually add water. Mix well.

Mix together all ingredients for dip and refrigerate.

Drain turkey pieces and dry well on kitchen paper. Heat oil in a deep-fryer. Coat turkey pieces in batter and deep-fry until golden and cooked right through. Drain on kitchen paper. Serve hot accompanied by coriander dip.

TURKEY AND SALAMI SPIRALS

8 slices wheatmeal
  bread
a little cooking oil
8oz (225g) turkey
  escalopes
1 ½oz (40g) dolcelatte,
  grated
1 ½oz (40g) thin slices
  salami
1 ½ tsp green
  peppercorns in brine,
  crushed
olive oil for brushing
several grapes

Remove crusts from bread and cut each slice into 3 rectangles. Brush both sides with a little oil. Place on a baking sheet and bake in a preheated 220°C (425°F) Gas 7 oven for about 10 minutes or until crisp and golden. Leave to cool.

Place turkey escalopes between sheets of cling film and flatten by beating with a rolling pin. Cover with cheese, then with salami. Sprinkle peppercorns over the top.

Roll up fillets, turkey side outmost. Secure with cocktail sticks and brush surfaces with olive oil. Bake in a preheated 170°C (325°F) Gas 3 oven for 20 minutes. Leave until cold.

Slice turkey spirals thinly on the slant and arrange on bread croutes. Cut slivers of grapes and use for garnishing. Cling film and store in a cool place until serving.

Meat & Venison

Sample this range of meaty morsels
that are succulent and flavoursome

(All recipes make or serve 24)

A well stocked delicatessen offers a wonderful variety of smoked and cured meats, sausages, salami and pâtés suitable for canapes. Add some interesting fillings and a garnish and with a minimal amount of effort the end result is pretty as well as delicious. The bresaola with boursin cheese is simply made but very effective, as are the salami rolls with beansprout and cucumber filling.

Fresh meats provide some tasty favourites, such as rich and creamy beef stroganoff en croute, or miniature Cornish pasties. Rare slices of beef fillet, pepper-rimmed and topped with fanned-out strawberries, or tender raw beef in steak tartar, topped with glowing little quail egg yolks, are for serious carnivores.

SALAMI TOWERS

24 slices black bread
2oz (50g) soft butter
9oz (250g) piece
   German salami,
   approx. 1½" (4cm) in
   diameter

5 tbsp finely chopped
   chives
4 hard-boiled eggs
8 pimento-stuffed olives
cayenne for dusting

U sing a small pastry cutter, cut out 24
rounds of bread. Butter thinly. Cut
salami into ¼" (0.5cm) thick slices.

Place a salami slice in centre of each
bread round. Dip the double-edge of each
slice in chives to cover all round. Cut each
egg into 6 slices and top each salami piece
with an egg slice. Slice each olive into 3 and
place a slice on top of each egg. Dust with a
little cayenne before serving.

PEPPERED BEEF WITH STRAWBERRY

1 lb (450g) beef fillet, in
  one piece
1 tbsp smooth Dijon
  mustard
1 tbsp mixed
  peppercorns (green,
  pink, white and
  black), crushed

24 slices wheatmeal
  bread
3 tbsp oil
24 small strawberries

Coat beef fillet with a thin layer of mustard. Press crushed peppercorns into beef. Place on a roasting tray and roast in a preheated 220°C (425°F) Gas 7 oven for 15–20 minutes. Set aside and leave to cool.

Using a small pastry cutter, cut bread into 24 rounds. Place on a baking sheet, brush with oil and bake in a preheated 220°C (425°F) Gas 7 oven for 10 minutes. Leave to cool.

Slice beef into thin slices and pile onto bread croutes. Slice strawberries, tip to base, without cutting right through. Spread out slices into a fan shape and place on croutes. Cling film and store in a cool place until serving.

STEAK TARTAR WITH QUAIL'S EGGS

24 slices white bread
3 tbsp cooking oil
12oz (350g) fillet or
  rump steak
seasoning
3 tbsp mayonnaise
2 tsp French mustard
1 tsp capers, finely
  chopped
24 small red onion rings
24 raw quail egg yolks

Using a small pastry cutter, cut out 24 rounds of bread. Place on a baking sheet, brush with oil and bake in a preheated 220°C (425°F) Gas 7 oven for 10 minutes. Leave to cool.

Mince beef finely and blend seasoning in well. Form into 24 small patties and set aside.

Blend together mayonnaise and mustard. Stir in capers. Spread bread croutes with the mixture. Place a beef patty on each bread croute. Make a small hollow in the centre of each patty, and surround with a small onion ring. Carefully slip an egg yolk into each hollow.

Prepare the steak tartar shortly before serving.

PORK AND BLACK BEAN PASTIES

6oz (175g) pork fillet
2 tbsp cooking oil
2 tbsp canned black beans in salted sauce (from Chinese supermarkets)
¾" (2cm) root ginger, very finely chopped
1 clove garlic, crushed
24 small wheat cake wrappers (from Chinese and Japanese supermarkets)
oil for deep-frying

Cut pork into very thin strips, about ½" (1cm) long. Heat oil in a frying pan and stir-fry pork very quickly. Remove from heat and add black beans, ginger and garlic. Mix thoroughly and leave until cold.

Fill wheat wrappers one at a time (keeping remainder covered to prevent drying out); place 1 tsp filling on one half of wrapper, leaving ¼" (0.5cm) round edge. Brush edge with water and fold wrapper in half, pressing edges together, to make a semi-circle.

Heat oil in a deep-fryer and cook pasties, a few at a time, until crisp and golden. Drain on kitchen paper. Serve hot or cold – if serving cold, cling film and store in a cool place until needed.

BEEF STROGANOFF EN CROUTE

12 slices white bread
a little cooking oil
12oz (350g) lean rump
  or sirloin steak
1½oz (40g) butter
2 shallots, finely
  chopped
6oz (175g) button
  mushrooms, thinly
  sliced
1 tbsp smooth Dijon
  mustard
3floz (75ml) soured
  cream
seasoning
12 black olives, sliced
paprika for dusting

Remove crusts from bread and cut each slice in half to form 24 triangles. Brush both sides with a little oil. Place on a baking sheet and bake in a preheated 220°C (425°F) Gas 7 oven for about 10 minutes or until crisp and golden. Leave to cool.

Place steak between two sheets of cling film and beat flat with a rolling pin. Cut meat into short thin strips. Heat ⅓ of butter in a pan and brown meat quickly over high heat. Set aside.

Heat remaining butter and cook shallots gently until soft and translucent. Add mushrooms and cook until soft. Turn up heat and continue cooking over high heat until liquid has evaporated. Stir in mustard.

Return meat to the pan and stir in soured cream. Season and heat through but do not boil. Spoon mixture onto croutes, garnish with olives and dust with a little paprika before serving.

BRESAOLA AND BOURSIN ON RYE

24 thin slices light rye bread
5oz (150g) black pepper boursin
1 floz (25ml) plain yogurt
24 slices bresaola (dry-cured Italian beef), approx. 5oz (150g)
small bunch chives, chopped into ½" (1cm) lengths

Using a small pastry cutter, cut bread into 24 rounds. Blend boursin with yogurt and spread over bread, reserving some for centres.

Pinch together the centre of each bresaola slice to form a cup shape and press the centre into bread. Divide remaining boursin between bresaola 'cups'. Stick chive lengths into centres for garnish.

The bread can be spread with boursin some time in advance, but bresaola should be added shortly before serving as it can dry out quite quickly.

DEVILLED TONGUE WITH GHERKINS

24 slices white bread
3 tbsp cooking oil
8oz (225g) sliced ox tongue
3oz (75g) gherkins, diced small
12floz (350ml) double cream
1 tbsp mustard powder
1 tsp green peppercorns in brine, crushed
finely chopped parsley for sprinkling

Line 24 small pastry cases with bread and trim edges with scissors. Brush with oil and bake in a preheated 220°C (425°F) Gas 7 oven for 10 minutes. Leave to cool.

Cut tongue into small, thin strips and mix with diced gherkin. Spoon mixture into bread cases.

Beat cream to a dropping consistency. Blend mustard with peppercorns and 1 tbsp cream, then mix into remaining cream.

Spoon over tongue and return to 220°C (425°F) Gas 7 oven for 5 minutes until top is golden brown. Sprinkle with parsley to garnish.

PORK WITH OLIVES AND RED PEPPER

9oz (250g) pork fillet
1 tbsp olive oil
1 shallot, finely
  chopped
1/2oz (15g) fresh
  breadcrumbs
1/2 tsp coriander
pinch thyme
1 tbsp quark
seasoning

12 green pimento-
  stuffed olives
1 1/2 tbsp paprika
12 long slices
  pumpernickel bread
soft butter for spreading
1 punnet mustard and
  cress
1/2 small red pepper

Cut a deep pocket into pork fillet
lengthwise, taking care not to cut right
through. Place opened-up between two
sheets of cling film and beat as flat as
possible with a rolling pin. Set aside.

Heat oil in a pan and cook shallot gently until soft and translucent. Add breadcrumbs, coriander and thyme. Remove from heat and leave to cool. Stir in quark.

Season flattened pork and spread cooled stuffing evenly over inside of meat. Place olives in a line down centre of meat. Roll up meat as neatly as possible and secure with string. Dust with paprika.

Cook meat, join downwards, covered with foil, in a preheated 180°C (350°F) Gas 4 oven for 45 minutes. Leave to cool. Remove string and slice meat as thinly as possible into 48 slices.

Cut out 24×2″ (5cm) squares of bread (by halving slices) and spread with butter. Top with mustard and cress. Add 2 pork slices, slightly overlapping. Cut red pepper into very thin slivers and pile a little in centre of each round.

LITTLE CORNISH PASTIES

*1 lb (450g) shortcrust
    pastry*
beaten egg for brushing

FILLING
3 tbsp cooking oil
*3 shallots, very finely
    chopped*
3oz (75g) potato, diced
*6oz (175g) rump steak,
    diced small*
*1 tbsp coarse-grain
    mustard*
pinch thyme
seasoning

Roll out pastry fairly thinly on a floured surface. Using a small pastry cutter, cut out 24 rounds. Set aside.

Heat oil in a frying pan. Add shallots and cook over low heat just long enough to soften. Add potato and cook for a couple of minutes, stirring frequently. Leave to cool.

When cool, mix in diced beef, mustard, thyme and seasoning. Divide filling between pastry rounds, leaving edges clear. Brush edges with a little water and pinch together to form a seam at the top. Crimp edges.

Place pastries on a baking sheet and brush with beaten egg. Bake in a preheated 180°C (350°F) Gas 4 oven for 8–10 minutes or until golden brown. Serve hot or warm.

SPARE RIBS WITH RUM AND GINGER

8 – 12 pork spare ribs,
approx. 2lb (900g)

MARINADE
2 tbsp soy sauce
4 tbsp apple juice
1 tbsp dark rum
2 tsp brown sugar
2 pieces stem ginger,
finely chopped
2 tbsp red wine vinegar

Ask your butcher to chop ribs into 2 or 3 pieces, according to length. Trim off excess fat. Place ribs in a shallow dish. Mix together marinade ingredients and pour over ribs. Leave to absorb flavours for 1 hour or so, turning ribs once in a while.

Line a roasting tray with foil. Place ribs in it and brush generously with marinade. Roast in a preheated 220°C (425°F) Gas 7 oven for 45 – 50 minutes, turning ribs often and brushing with marinade. Serve hot or cold.

CASSLER AND PICKLED PEAR ON RYE

2 firm Conference
pears

FOR PICKLING PEARS
4 tbsp red wine vinegar
2 tbsp water
6 cloves
4 tsp brown sugar
2 tbsp finely chopped
red onion

FOR SERVING
24 slices soft black rye
bread
2–3 tbsp cooking oil
4 tbsp soured cream
1 tbsp smooth Dijon
mustard
24 thin slices cassler or
German smoked
ham, approx. 10oz
(275g)
tiny thyme sprigs

Peel, core and dice pears. Place vinegar, water, cloves and sugar in a pan. Gently bring to boil. When boiling, plunge in pears, reduce heat to simmering and cook until pears are soft. Add red onion. Remove pan from heat and leave pears and onion to cool in vinegar mixture.

Line 24 small pastry cases with bread slices and trim edges with scissors. Brush lightly with oil and bake in a preheated 220°C (425°F) Gas 7 oven for 8–10 minutes. Leave to cool.

Blend together soured cream and mustard. Arrange cassler in bread cases, and spoon cream mixture into centre. Top with diced pickled pear and onion, then garnish with thyme. Cling film and store in a cool place until serving.

SWEET AND SOUR KEBABS

10–12oz (275–350g)
  pork fillet
2 large yellow peppers
2 tsp sesame oil for
  grilling

MARINADE
3 tbsp soy sauce
2 tbsp medium sherry
2 tsp red wine vinegar
1 heaped tsp brown
  sugar
1 clove garlic, crushed

Cut pork into 24 cubes, approx. ½" (1cm). Cut pepper into 48 pieces. Place pork and pepper pieces in a shallow bowl. Blend together marinade ingredients and pour over pork and peppers. Leave to absorb flavours for 1 hour or so, turning pieces once in a while.

Thread pork and pepper onto a few wooden skewers for grilling. Brush with sesame oil and grill under a medium heat for 10–12 minutes, turning skewers every so often and brushing with remaining oil.

Remove meat and peppers from skewers and thread onto cocktail sticks for serving, with 1 piece pork and 2 pieces pepper on each. Serve hot or cold – if serving cold, cling film and store in a cool place until serving.

PÂTÉ WITH SAUTÉED OYSTER MUSHROOMS

14oz–1lb (400–450g)
  smooth liver pâté
24 slices white bread
3 tbsp cooking oil
1oz (25g) butter
6oz (175g) oyster
  mushrooms, torn into
  strips
1 tbsp finely chopped
  chives
seasoning
paprika for dusting
flat-leaved parsley

Place pâté in the freezer until very firm but not frozen. Slice into ¼" (0.5cm) slices, then cut out diamonds (or any other shape of your choice) using a pastry cutter. Cling film and refrigerate.

Using the same shape cutter as for the pâté but one size larger, cut bread into diamonds. Place on a baking sheet, brush with oil and bake in a preheated 220°C (425°F) Gas 7 oven for 10 minutes. Cool.

Meanwhile, heat butter in a frying pan. Add mushrooms and cook over fairly high heat, turning mushrooms frequently. When cooked, add chives and seasoning. Cool.

Dust very edges of croutes with paprika and place a pâté diamond on each. Top with a few slivers of mushroom, and parsley.

BACON ROLLS WITH APPLE STUFFING

24 slices sweet-cured,
  rindless, streaky
  bacon
2 tbsp cooking oil
7oz (200g) finely
  chopped onion
3oz (75g) grated
  cooking apple

2oz (50g) sultanas,
  chopped
12 sage leaves,
  chopped
black pepper

Stretch bacon rashers over back of a
knife. Heat oil in a pan and gently cook
onion until soft and translucent. Add
remaining ingredients and cook a little
longer. Cool.

Spread about 1 tsp filling over each
bacon rasher. Roll up and secure with
cocktail sticks.

In a non-stick frying pan, fry bacon rolls
until crisp and golden, turning frequently –
about 10 minutes over medium heat. Drain
on kitchen paper and remove cocktail sticks.
Serve hot or cold.

SALAMI AND BEANSPROUT ROLLS

3oz (75g) garlic-
 flavoured boursin
2 tbsp Greek yogurt
24 slices cervalet or
 other salami, approx.
 4oz (100g)

2oz (50g) cucumber
4 thin spring onions
3oz (75g) beansprouts

B lend together boursin and yogurt. Spread
mixture over sliced cervalet.
 Cut cucumber into thin batons. Cut
spring onions into 1″ (2.5cm) lengths then
lengthwise into slivers.
 Divide cucumber, spring onion and
beansprouts between slices of cervalet,
allowing vegetables to protrude a little at
ends. Roll up cervalet into tight little rolls.
Cling film and store in a cool place until
serving.

LAMB KOFTAS WITH MINT YOGURT DIP

2oz (50g) dried
  apricots
12oz (350g) very lean
  lamb
1 onion, finely chopped
2 tbsp chopped
  coriander
pinch allspice
small pinch chilli
seasoning
oil for frying
24 small mint leaves

DIP
7floz (200ml) Greek
  yogurt
1 clove garlic, crushed
1 tbsp lemon juice
1 tbsp finely chopped
  mint
salt

Soak apricots in a little water for a couple of hours. Drain and chop very finely. Set aside.

Trim lamb of any fat. Put through a mincer twice, the second time with onion. Alternatively, cut meat into pieces and reduce to fine mince in a food processor, adding onion towards the end.

Place meat in a bowl. Add apricots, coriander and spices, and season. Work ingredients together with your hands. Form mixture into 24 balls. (Wetting your hands slightly prevents meat from sticking to them.)

Heat oil in a frying pan. Add koftas, a few at a time, and brown well until cooked through, about 10 minutes. Shake pan from time to time to ensure even browning and nice, round koftas. Remove from pan and drain on kitchen paper. Serve hot or cold.

Just before serving, blend together dip ingredients and spoon into a shallow bowl. Serve koftas on cocktail sticks, topped with mint leaves, standing in dip.

KIDNEY AND MUSHROOM KEBABS

4 lamb's kidneys
3 tbsp red wine
1 clove garlic, crushed
seasoning
24 small button
mushrooms
3 tbsp olive oil
black pepper

Halve kidneys and remove centre core and gristle. Cut each half into 3 pieces, lengthwise, and wash well in cold water. Place in a bowl and add wine, garlic and seasoning. Leave to marinate for ½ hour.

Thread each piece of kidney, concertina fashion, onto a tiny skewer. Top each with a button mushroom. Brush with olive oil and cook under a high grill for about 5 minutes, turning frequently. Grind black pepper over and serve while still warm.

LAMB IN PASTRY CRESCENTS

FILLING
6oz (175g) very lean
   lamb, off bone
1 tbsp oil
½ onion, finely
   chopped
1 clove garlic, crushed
½" (1cm) root ginger,
   grated
2 tbsp finely chopped
   coriander
seasoning

PASTRY
12oz (350g) puff pastry
1 egg, beaten
2 tbsp cumin seeds

Cut lamb into short thin strips. Heat oil in a frying pan and cook onion until soft and translucent. Add lamb and brown very quickly, stirring all the time. Stir in garlic, ginger and coriander and season well. Remove from heat and leave to cool.

Roll out puff pastry thinly on a floured surface. Cut out 24×2" (5cm) squares. Divide filling between squares, about 1 tsp on each. Brush edges with beaten egg. Roll up filled pastry squares from one corner to the opposite one. Shape resulting rolls into crescents.

Place crescents on a dampened baking sheet. Brush with egg and sprinkle with cumin seeds. Bake in a preheated 200°C (400°F) Gas 6 oven for 20 minutes. Serve while hot.

SAUTÉED LAMB'S KIDNEYS EN CROUTE

4 lamb's kidneys

MARINADE
4 tbsp dry sherry
pinch thyme

FOR SERVING
6 slices white bread
3 tbsp cooking oil

TOPPING
3oz (75g) streaky
    bacon, diced small
1 onion, very finely
    chopped
pinch allspice
seasoning
1 tsp cornflour
4 tbsp double cream
2 tbsp finely chopped
    parsley

Halve kidneys, remove centre core and gristle and wash in cold water. Slice thinly across and place in a bowl. Pour over sherry, sprinkle with thyme and leave to marinate for ½ hour.

Meanwhile, remove crusts from bread and, using a small oval pastry cutter, cut 24 ovals from bread. Place on a baking sheet, brush with oil and bake in a preheated 220°C (425°F) Gas 7 oven for 10 minutes. Leave to cool.

Heat a frying pan. Add bacon and cook, stirring frequently, to draw out fat. Turn down heat, add onion and cook until soft and translucent. Drain kidneys, reserving marinade. Add kidneys to the frying pan and cook over high heat until browned. Add allspice and seasoning. Dilute cornflour in reserved marinade and stir into kidneys. Cook until juices thicken, then stir in cream and heat through gently.

Divide kidneys between bread croutes. Top with chopped parsley and serve hot.

VENISON AND CRANBERRY PATTIES

2oz (50g) cranberries
4 tbsp unsweetened
  orange juice
12oz (350g) venison
  sausages
pinch thyme
8 juniper berries,
  crushed
24 slices wheatmeal
  bread
2–3 tbsp cooking oil
1 small bag matchstick
  potato chips

P lace cranberries and orange juice in a small pan. Bring to boil and cook very gently until berries are just soft. Leave to cool.

Remove and discard skins from sausages. Place meat in a bowl. Add thyme, juniper and cold cranberries. Mix well. Shape mixture into 24 small patties and set aside.

Remove crusts and cut bread into 24×1½″ (4cm) squares. Place on a baking sheet, brush lightly with oil and bake in a preheated 220°C (425°F) Gas oven for 10 minutes. Leave to cool.

Meanwhile, cook patties under a medium-hot grill until nice and golden and cooked right through – about 5–6 minutes, turning them a couple of times during cooking. Place a patty on top of each bread croute and top with a few halved potato matchsticks. Serve hot.

Eggs & Cheese

Treat your guests to a tempting selection of luscious cheese and egg delights

(All recipes make or serve 24)

Egg and cheese are popular and infinitely versatile ingredients for canapés. Most of the egg canapés here are served cold and can be prepared well ahead, a convenient aspect when catering for large numbers of guests. Quail eggs, just perfect in size, look enchanting and feature several times. Devilled, fried and served on beds of bright green spinach, or pickled and pale olive in colour – all are delectable.

Cheesy temptations, on the whole, are served hot, preferably straight from the grill or oven. Try tiny kebabs with bread croutes and smoked mozzarella, rarebit – an old favourite revamped with goat's cheese and olives – or grilled dolcelatte cheese and pears, an original and delightful combination.

FILLED EGG HALVES

18 hard-boiled eggs

FILLING 1
*4 black olives, finely
   chopped*
2 tsp plain yogurt
1 tsp olive oil
1 tsp soy sauce
black pepper
*a few chopped olives for
   garnish*

FILLING 2
pinch saffron
1 tbsp mayonnaise
salt
*chopped chives for
   garnish*

FILLING 3
1 tbsp taramosalata
*1 tbsp red lumpfish roe,
   plus extra for garnish*

Halve eggs. Discard whites (or use in a salad) from 6 eggs to leave 24. Place yolks in a bowl and mash until smooth with a fork. Divide into 3 equal parts. Mix each part with a different filling mixture. Using either a spoon or a piping bag, fill egg halves with fillings, and garnish appropriately. Cling film and refrigerate until ready to serve.

PICKLED QUAIL'S EGGS

24 quail's eggs

FOR PICKLING EGGS
1 1/2pt (900ml) water
4 tsp salt
1 tsp caraway seeds
1 tbsp crushed allspice
  berries
1 red onion, sliced
1 tbsp lemon juice

DIP
1/4pt (150ml) Greek
  yogurt
3 tbsp smooth Dijon
  mustard
2 tbsp finely chopped
  chives

Place all pickling ingredients in a pan.
Bring to boil and simmer for 5 minutes.
Leave to cool, then strain away spices and
onion.

Boil quail's eggs for 3 minutes. Plunge
into cold water and shell when cool. Place
eggs in a jar with a lid, pour pickling liquid
over them and leave for 2–3 days before
using.

Blend together dip ingredients and
serve with pickled eggs.

DEVILLED QUAIL'S EGGS WITH CAPERS

12 quail's eggs
24 slices wheatmeal
   bread
3 tbsp cooking oil
8floz (225ml) double
   cream

1 tbsp Dijon mustard
1 ½ tsp chilli sauce
   (from Chinese
   supermarkets)
2 tsp finely chopped
   capers

Boil quail's eggs for 3 minutes. Plunge into cold water and shell when cool.

Line 24 small pastry cases with bread and trim edges with scissors. Brush with oil and bake in a preheated 220°C (425°F) Gas 7 oven for 10 minutes. Leave to cool.

Whip cream to a dropping consistency. Blend in mustard, chilli sauce and capers.

Halve eggs and place a half in each bread case. Spoon over cream mixture and cook in a preheated 250°C (475°F) Gas 9 oven for 5 minutes. Serve as soon as they are cooked.

MARBLED EGGS IN TAPENADE

12 small eggs

FOR COOKING EGGS
2 tbsp black China tea
3floz (75ml) dark soy
*   sauce*
2 star-anise

TAPENADE
¹/₂oz (15g) anchovy
*   fillets*
3floz (75ml) milk
2oz (50g) black olives,
*   stoned*
2oz (50g) canned tuna
1 tbsp olive oil
1 small clove garlic,
*   crushed*
1 tbsp brandy
black pepper

FOR SERVING
24 slices brown bread,
*   toasted*
mustard and cress or
*   alfalfa*

Hard-boil eggs. Cool. Crack shells as evenly as possible by tapping them with the back of a heavy spoon. Place cracked eggs in a saucepan with tea, soy sauce and star anise, and enough water to cover eggs.

Bring to boil and simmer for 1 hour, topping up water if necessary, so that eggs are always covered. Leave eggs to cool in the liquid. Carefully peel away shells to reveal marbled pattern, then halve eggs lengthwise.

For tapenade, soak anchovies in milk for 10 minutes. Drain and place anchovies with all other tapenade ingredients in a food processor and process until completely smooth.

Using an oval pastry cutter about ½″ (1cm) larger than base of halved eggs, cut out 24 ovals from toasted bread. Spread toast with a little tapenade, cover with a few sprigs of mustard and cress or alfalfa, top with halved eggs and serve.

FRIED QUAIL'S EGG ON SPINACH

24 slices white bread
3 tbsp olive oil
10oz (275g) trimmed
    tender spinach leaves
2¹/₂oz (65g) butter
2 spring onions, thinly
    sliced
2 tbsp soured cream
seasoning
24 quail's eggs

Push bread into 24 small square pastry cases. Trim edges with scissors. Brush with olive oil and bake in a preheated 220°C (425°F) Gas 7 oven for 10 minutes. Leave to cool.

Wash spinach well and shred finely. Heat 1oz (25g) of butter in a pan. Add spinach and spring onions and cook gently until spinach is just soft, adding a little water if necessary. Drain away excess water from spinach.

Blend soured cream and seasoning into spinach. Fill bread cases with mixture.

Heat remaining butter in a non-stick frying pan and fry quail's eggs over low heat, a few at a time, until whites are just set. Place a quail's egg in each bread case, trimming the edges a little if necessary. Serve warm.

SCRAMBLED EGG WITH SMOKED SALMON

24 slices white bread
3 tbsp cooking oil
4 eggs
4floz (100ml) single
    cream
seasoning
1½oz (40g) butter
3oz (75g) smoked
    salmon, cut into very
    thin strips
1 tbsp finely chopped
    chives

Using a small round pastry cutter, cut out 24 rounds of bread. Place on a baking sheet, brush with oil and bake in a preheated 220°C (425°F) Gas 7 oven for 10 minutes. Leave to cool.

Lightly beat eggs and cream together. Season. In a heavy pan, melt butter over low heat. Turn up heat a little, add egg mixture and cook, pushing mixture away from base of pan as it begins to set. Before all mixture is set, remove from heat and keep stirring a little longer, as egg will continue to cook from heat of pan.

Spoon scrambled egg onto bread croutes. Garnish with slivers of salmon and chopped chives.

FILLED OMELETTE SPIRALS

OMELETTES
6 eggs
3 tbsp water
seasoning
oil for frying

FILLING
4–5oz (100–150g)
  boursin with herbs
3 tbsp Greek yogurt
4oz (100g) alfalfa
  sprouts

FOR SERVING
1–1½ cucumbers, cut
  on the slant into ¼"
  (0.5cm) thick slices
2oz (50g) black
  lumpfish roe
mustard and cress

Beat eggs with water and season. Heat a
little oil in a non-stick frying pan. Make
6 thin omelettes with egg mixture, cooking
them on one side only. Stack them on top of
each other as they are cooked, placing a
piece of greaseproof paper between each
layer. Leave to cool.

Blend boursin with yogurt. Place an
omelette on a flat surface, spread with a
little cheese mixture, scatter with alfalfa,
place another omelette on top and repeat
layers of cheese and alfalfa. Roll up as tightly
as possible. Repeat with the remaining
omelettes, forming 3 rolls altogether. Place
in the refrigerator to 'set' for at least ½ hour.

Cut omelette rolls into slices, slicing
them on the slant. Using a cucumber slice as
a base, place an omelette slice on top. Spoon
a little black lumpfish roe into centre of
omelette slice and garnish with mustard and
cress. Cling film and store in a cool place
until ready to serve.

QUARK AND HAZELNUT PASTRIES

5oz (150g) puff pastry
1oz (25g) hazelnuts
1oz (25g) sultanas
1oz (25g) quark
2 tbsp soured cream
1/2 egg, beaten

Roll out pastry on a floured surface into a rectangle approx. 14×5″ (35×12cm). Place nuts, sultanas, quark and soured cream in a food processor and process briefly. Spread mixture over rolled-out pastry.

Roll from longer end into a swiss roll shape. Trim very ends and discard. Slice roll into 24 equal pieces. Place these cartwheels on a dampened baking sheet, brush with beaten egg and bake in a preheated 200°C (400°F) Gas 6 oven for 7–8 minutes until golden. Serve while still warm.

LITTLE SCOTCH EGGS

24 quail's eggs
2 tbsp seasoned flour
12oz (350g) high-
quality sausages
2 tbsp very finely
chopped parsley
2 eggs, beaten
1½–2oz (40–50g)
fine oatmeal
oil for deep-frying

Boil quail's eggs for 3 minutes. Plunge into cold water and shell when cool. Roll in seasoned flour.

Skin sausages and place meat in a bowl. Mix with parsley. Divide meat into 24 portions and flatten into rounds. Place an egg in the centre of each portion and work meat round egg as evenly as possible, ensuring that the surface is free from cracks.

Brush meat-covered eggs with beaten egg. Roll in oatmeal until coated.

Heat oil in a deep-fryer and cook Scotch eggs for 5–6 minutes until golden and the sausagemeat is cooked right through. (It is important not to have the oil too hot. When a bread cube browns in 40–50 seconds, the oil is the correct temperature.) Drain eggs on kitchen paper and serve hot or cold.

EGGS IN CURRIED BÉCHAMEL

24 slices wheatmeal
  bread
3 tbsp cooking oil
1½oz (40g) butter
1½oz (40g) plain flour
1 tsp hot curry powder
¾pt (450ml) milk
2 tbsp chopped
  coriander
6 hard-boiled eggs,
  shelled
seasoning
coriander leaves

Push bread into 24 small pastry cases and trim edges with scissors. Brush with oil and bake in a preheated 220°C (425°F) Gas 7 oven for 10 minutes. Leave to cool.

Meanwhile make béchamel sauce. Melt butter in a pan, stir in flour and curry powder and cook over low heat for a couple of minutes, stirring all the time. Remove from heat. Heat milk until almost boiling and gradually stir into flour mixture. Return to heat. Bring to boil and simmer for a couple of minutes, stirring all the time. Remove from heat and add coriander.

Reserve 3 hard-boiled egg yolks. Chop remainder of eggs finely and add to sauce. Season. Spoon mixture into bread cases.

Chop reserved egg yolk finely and sprinkle on top. Garnish with coriander and serve while still warm.

PANCAKE PARCELS WITH HAM AND CHEESE

BATTER
5oz (150g) self-raising flour
pinch salt
1 large egg
13floz (375ml) skimmed milk
oil for frying

FILLING
2¹/₂oz (65g) smoked ham, diced small
2¹/₂oz (65g) cheddar, grated
1 tbsp coarse-grain Dijon mustard
2 tbsp chopped watercress

Sift flour and salt into a bowl. Beat egg with 2 tbsp of milk and stir into flour mixture. Add remainder of milk gradually, stirring all the time. Rest batter for ½ hour.

Mix together ham, cheese, mustard and watercress in a bowl.

Heat a little oil in a frying pan. Spoon in enough batter to make a thin 3″ (7.5cm) pancake. Cook pancake on one side only. Repeat until batter is used up, piling pancakes onto a plate, separated by small squares of greaseproof paper.

When all pancakes are cooked, place 1 tbsp of filling in centre of each. Fold over edges to make a neat parcel. Fry the parcels quickly, folded side first to seal the edges. Serve hot or cold.

OATMEAL PANCAKES WITH CREAMY FISH ROE

BATTER
I small egg
½pt (300ml) milk
¼ tsp bicarbonate of
   soda
pinch salt
3 – 3½oz (75 – 90g)
   fine-ground oatmeal
a little butter or
   margarine for frying

TOPPING
¼pt (150ml) soured
   cream
I heaped tbsp finely
   chopped chives
I small jar salmon roe
chervil sprigs

Beat together egg and milk. In a bowl, mix bicarbonate, salt and oatmeal. Stir in egg liquid, a little at a time, mixing well. Leave to stand for 15 minutes.

Heat a little butter or margarine in a frying pan. Drop batter, about 1 tbsp at a time, onto the pan. Cook pancakes over medium heat, a couple of minutes either side. (Stir the standing batter frequently while cooking the pancakes.)

When cool, top pancakes with 1 tsp soured cream, a little roe and chervil to garnish. Serve warm.

RACHEL'S CHOUX RINGS WITH SALMON PÂTÉ

CHOUX PASTRY
3oz (75g) butter
4½floz (125ml) water
3½oz (90g) plain flour,
  sifted
2½oz (65g) grated
  parmesan

3 eggs
1½ tsp cayenne

FILLING
8oz (225g) ready-made
  smoked salmon pâté

Place butter and water in a saucepan. Heat gently until butter has melted, then bring to boil. Remove from heat and add flour and parmesan, beating into the mixture with a wooden spoon. Return to heat and continue beating until mixture is smooth and forms a ball. Remove from heat, beat in eggs a little at a time, and finally add cayenne. Beat until glossy and very smooth.

Pipe into rings (approx. 1½"/4cm in diameter) on a dampened baking sheet. The mixture should make 48 rings. Bake in a preheated 200°C (400°F) Gas 6 oven for 8–9 minutes. Pierce rings in a couple of places when baked, to allow steam to escape.

Leave until just cool, then spread salmon pâté over half the number of rings and sandwich the rings together in pairs.

Serve as soon as possible after filling. If preparing the choux rings beforehand, they can be piped and then frozen before cooking. Thaw thoroughly before cooking or the rings won't rise.

CURD CHEESE ON TORTILLA CHIPS

6oz (175g) curd cheese
3 heaped tbsp finely
    chopped chives
2 tsp paprika

1oz (25g) pistachio
    nuts, finely chopped
24 pine kernels, toasted
24 tortilla chips

Divide curd cheese into 3 equal portions. Form into tiny balls. Roll balls in the 3 different coatings: paprika, chopped chives and pistachio nuts. Flatten balls slightly and press a pine kernel into the top of each. Place balls inside tortilla chips and serve.

SMOKED MOZZARELLA KEBABS

12oz (350g) smoked mozzarella
4–6 thick slices white bread
4 tbsp olive oil

Cut mozzarella into 24 cubes. Remove crusts and cut each bread slice into 4–6 squares, to make 48 cubes approx. ¾" (2cm). Thread 1 cheese and 2 bread cubes onto 24 tiny skewers, placing cheese between bread.

Brush with oil. Place under a hot grill and cook just long enough for bread to brown and cheese to begin to soften. (Take care not to overcook.) Serve as soon as possible.

MEDITERRANEAN RAREBIT

4 slices wheatmeal
  bread
8oz (225g) goat's
  cheese
12 black olives, finely
  chopped
1 tsp mustard powder
1/2 tsp cayenne
1 tsp lemon juice
4 tbsp dry white wine

Toast bread on one side only. Place remaining ingredients in a saucepan and cook until soft and runny. Allow mixture to cool a little.

Spread mixture over untoasted side of bread. Place under a preheated hot grill and cook until golden brown and bubbly. Cut each slice into 6 pieces and serve while hot.

FILO POUCHES WITH FETA

6oz (175g) feta
1 tbsp finely chopped
    coriander
6 black olives, chopped
2 tsp pine kernels
black pepper
4 sheets filo pastry,
    approx. 12×8″
    (30×20cm)
olive oil for brushing

Blend together feta, coriander, olives and pine kernels. Season with pepper.

Work with 1 sheet of pastry at a time, keeping rest covered with cling film to prevent drying out. Brush uppermost side of filo with oil and fold in half, forming a rectangle 6×8″ (15×20cm). Brush surface with oil. Cut into 6 equal pieces by halving lengthwise then cutting across into thirds.

Place some filling in centre of each piece of pastry. Gather edges together, twisting top to form a pouch shape. Brush all over with olive oil. Repeat with the other sheets of filo and filling mixture.

Place cheese pouches on an oiled baking sheet and bake in a preheated 200°C (400°F) Gas 6 oven for 10 minutes. Serve hot (they can also be made in advance and reheated before serving).

DOLCELATTE AND PEARS EN CROUTE

8 slices white bread
¹/₂oz (15g) soft butter
I large, slightly firm
  pear, peeled

24 large tarragon
  leaves
6oz (175g) dolcelatte,
  sliced thinly

Remove crusts from bread and cut each
slice into 3 rectangles. Butter bread
lightly. Quarter pear then slice it fairly
thinly. Place 2 tarragon leaves on each piece
of buttered bread, arrange a pear slice on top
and cover with dolcelatte.

Place croutes on a baking sheet and bake
in a preheated 220°C (425°F) Gas 7 oven for
10 minutes. Serve while still warm.

PIZZA BITES WITH OREGANO

DOUGH
1 ½ tsp dried yeast
1 tbsp warm water
4oz (100g) strong plain
  flour
pinch salt
1 tbsp olive oil
1 tbsp milk
olive oil for greasing

TOPPING
½ tsp oregano, crushed
seasoning
6oz (175g) mozzarella,
  sliced
1 can anchovy fillets,
  drained and cut into
  slivers
6–8 black olives,
  halved and cut into
  slivers

Blend yeast with water. Sift flour and salt into a bowl. Make a well in centre and pour in yeast, oil and milk. Mix to a fairly firm but not stiff dough, adding a little more milk if necessary.

Turn onto a floured board and knead dough thoroughly. Place in a clean bowl and leave in a warm place until risen and doubled in size.

Turn out dough and knead lightly. Divide into 24 equal pieces. Push dough into oiled 1¾" (4.5cm) square pastry cases. Brush surface with a little oil.

Sprinkle dough with oregano and seasoning, and cover with mozzarella. Place pizzas in a preheated 190°C (375°F) Gas 5 oven and cook for 7 minutes. Top pizzas with anchovy and olives, return to oven and bake for a further 5 minutes. Serve while still hot.

Fruits & Vegetables

*Fill a platter with a colourful array
of fresh and fruity mouthfuls*

(All recipes make or serve 24)

Even in fairly modest supermarkets, a wealth of exotic fruit and vegetables are constantly on offer. Colourful and pretty, they provide the perfect base for a number of canapés. A few of the recipes given here are vegetarian, but most include meat or fish in the ingredients.

Many fruit and vegetables make ideal little containers for holding fillings. Boat-shaped mange-tout are used here as vessels for crab meat, and hollowed-out cherry tomatoes are filled to the brim with tiny, brown shrimps. Button mushrooms, stalks removed, reveal hollows just large enough to hold herb- and garlic-laden snails. And for a fiery touch try chillies, of the milder kind, with a diced chicken stuffing.

FRIED TOFU TOPPED WITH SEAWEED

9oz (250g) tofu
1 tbsp soy sauce
1 tbsp medium-dry sherry
1 tsp sesame oil
6 tbsp cooking oil for frying
1 small cucumber
½ sheet nori seaweed
4 spring onions, very finely sliced

Cut tofu into 1–1¼″ (2.5–3cm) squares, ½″ (1cm) thick. Place in a shallow dish. Mix together soy sauce, sherry and sesame oil. Pour over tofu and leave for at least 1 hour, turning pieces once in a while.

Drain tofu well on kitchen paper. Heat oil in a non-stick frying pan. Fry tofu until golden brown on both sides. Leave to cool.

Slice cucumber into 24 pieces. Place a tofu cube onto each cucumber slice.

Toast nori seaweed under a medium grill until iridescent in appearance, taking care not to burn it. Shred toasted nori finely with scissors.

Top tofu pieces with nori and finely sliced spring onions. Cling film and store in a cool place until ready to serve.

Devils on Horseback

24 large prunes, stoned
1/4pt (150ml) port
  (optional)
5oz (150g) stilton
2 tbsp fromage frais
2 tbsp chopped
  hazelnuts

12 slices streaky bacon,
  approx. 6oz (175g)
12 slices wheatmeal
  bread

Soak prunes in port (or water if preferred) for ½ hour or so.

Blend together stilton, fromage frais and hazelnuts. Drain prunes and fill with cheese mixture. Cut bacon into 24 long thin strips and wrap a piece around each prune. Secure bacon on with cocktail sticks.

Grill under preheated medium heat until bacon is crisp and golden. Remove the cocktail sticks.

Remove crusts and cut bread into 24×1½″ (4cm) squares. Toast on both sides. Place a bacon-wrapped prune on top of each piece of toast. Serve while still warm.

APRICOTS WITH FETA AND PINE NUTS

12 ripe, sweet apricots
a little lemon juice
4oz (100g) feta, finely
    crumbled
4 tbsp Greek yogurt

2 tsp finely chopped
    basil
2 tsp olive oil
2 tbsp pine kernels

Halve apricots and remove stones. Hollow
out the centres a little and brush
surfaces with a little lemon juice to prevent
discolouration. Mix together feta, yogurt,
basil and olive oil. Fill apricots with mixture.

Toast pine kernels in a hot frying pan,
shaking the pan all the time until kernels are
lightly golden. Stick pine kernels into apricot
filling and serve.

EXOTIC SALAD IN CURRY MAYONNAISE

1 tbsp cooking oil
1 tsp hot curry powder
1 tbsp lemon juice
4 tbsp Greek yogurt
4 tbsp mayonnaise
24 slices white bread
3 tbsp cooking oil
1 paw paw
2 avocados
1 tbsp finely chopped
  coriander
24 pistachio nuts,
  chopped

Heat oil gently. Add curry powder and cook briefly. Add lemon juice and cook a little longer. Remove from heat and leave to cool. Blend in yogurt and mayonnaise.

Line 24 small round or oval pastry cases with bread slices. Trim edges with scissors. Brush with oil and bake in a preheated 220°C (425°F) Gas 7 oven for 10 minutes. Cool.

Cut paw paw and avocado into small dice and blend with coriander into yogurt.

Spoon fruit mixture into bread cases. Top with chopped nuts. Cling film and store in a cool place until serving.

STAR FRUIT WITH SMOKED TROUT

24 slices white bread
3 tbsp cooking oil
4 tbsp mayonnaise
finely chopped chives
6oz (175g) smoked
    trout
4 tbsp hot horseradish
    relish
black pepper
3 small star fruits
seeds from ½
    pomegranate

Remove crusts and cut bread into 24×2″ (5cm) squares. Place on a baking sheet, brush with oil and bake in a preheated 220°C (425°F) Gas 7 oven for 10 minutes. Leave to cool.

Spread 1 tbsp mayonnaise over bread croutes and dip surfaces in chopped chives.

Flake smoked trout into a bowl, removing any bones. Mix together remaining mayonnaise and horseradish. Season with pepper. Fold mayonnaise mixture into trout and set aside.

Cut each star fruit into 8 slices. Place a slice on each bread croute. Pile trout into centre of star fruit and top with a few pomegranate seeds. Cling film and store in a cool place until serving.

APPLE RINGS WITH GOAT'S CHEESE

24 slices wheatmeal
  bread
3 tbsp cooking oil
6 medium Cox's apples,
  peeled if preferred

1 tbsp olive oil
1 tbsp lemon juice
6–7oz (175–200g)
  goat's cheese
black pepper

Using a small round pastry cutter, cut out 24 rounds from bread. Place on a baking sheet, brush with oil and bake in a preheated 220°C (425°F) Gas 7 oven for 8 minutes. Leave to cool.

Meanwhile, cut off top and bottom of apples and core them. Slice each apple into 4 equal rings. Mix olive oil with lemon juice and brush over apple rings. Place one on each bread croute.

Crumble goat's cheese and pile into centre of apples. Grind some black pepper over the top. Grill under high heat for 5 minutes or until cheese is melting and changing colour.

MELON IN SALAMI WRAPPING

6 slices soft, black
  bread
1/2oz (15g) soft butter
4 tbsp finely chopped
  chives

I small, ripe melon
24 slices pepper salami,
  approx. 4oz (100g)

Cut crusts off bread. Butter bread and
divide chives between slices. Cut each
slice into 4 squares and set aside.

   Halve melon and scoop out seeds. Use a
melon baller to make 24 ball shapes.

   Thread each bread cube onto a cocktail
stick, chive side uppermost. Wrap a salami
slice round each melon ball and thread onto
the cocktail stick. Cling film and store in a
cool place until serving.

BAKED AVOCADO TOPPED WITH CRAB

24 slices wheatmeal
  bread
2¹/₂oz (65g) butter
1oz (25g) flour
¹/₂pt (300ml) milk
8oz (225g) cooked
  white crab meat

seasoning
3 avocados
2–3 tbsp grated
  parmesan
a little oil for brushing
chervil sprigs

Using a small round pastry cutter, cut out 24 rounds from bread. Lightly spread 1½oz (40g) butter on to bread. Set aside.

Place remaining butter and flour in a saucepan. Cook for a couple of minutes, stirring all the time. Heat milk in another pan to almost boiling. Take off heat and stir gradually into butter/flour mixture. Bring to boil and simmer gently for a couple of minutes. Add crab meat and seasoning.

Quarter avocados lengthwise, remove skin and cut them across into slices. Place avocado slices in a circle along outer rim of each bread round to form a hollow in the centre. Pile crab into the hollow and sprinkle on parmesan. Oil avocado lightly.

Place on a lightly oiled baking sheet and bake in a preheated 220°C (425°F) Gas 7 oven for 10–15 minutes until cheese is golden brown. Garnish with chervil and serve while still warm.

137

KIWIFRUIT WITH PEPPERED MACKEREL

24 slices white bread
3 tbsp cooking oil
4 tbsp mayonnaise
2 tsp coarse-grain
  mustard
12oz (350g) smoked
  peppered mackerel
2 kiwifruits, peeled and
  sliced

Using a small oval pastry cutter, cut out 24 ovals from bread. Push bread into 24 small round pastry cases, so that you end up with boat-shaped bread cases. Brush with oil and bake in a preheated 220°C (425°F) Gas 7 oven for 10 minutes. Leave to cool.

Blend together mayonnaise and mustard. Flake mackerel and fold into mayonnaise. Pile fish mixture into centre of croutes. Top with kiwi slices cut into quarters. Cling film and store in a cool place until serving.

FRESH FRUITS DIPPED IN SALT AND CHILLI

4 firm peaches, halved
2 Chinese pears, halved
   and cored
4 bananas
6 tbsp lemon juice
2 tbsp sea salt
1 1/2 tsp chilli
3 tbsp chopped
   coriander

Cut peaches and Chinese pears into thin slices. Place in a shallow bowl. Slice bananas on the slant and add to other fruits. Pour over lemon juice and leave to stand for 10–15 minutes.

Meanwhile, crush sea salt with chilli powder. Drain sliced fruits and dry on kitchen paper. Sprinkle both sides of fruit with salt/chilli mixture, then with chopped coriander. Prepare shortly before serving.

CHERRY TOMATOES WITH SHRIMPS

24 firm cherry
  tomatoes
10oz (275g) shelled
  brown shrimps
1 tbsp lemon juice
1 tsp grated lemon rind
2 tbsp finely chopped
  chervil

pinch cayenne
2 tbsp mayonnaise
1 small clove garlic,
  crushed
seasoning

Cut a tiny lid from each tomato and
reserve. Carefully scoop out seeds from
tomatoes and discard. Place tomatoes
upside down on kitchen paper to drain off
excess liquid.

Meanwhile, prepare filling. Place shrimps
in a bowl and stir in all the other ingredients.
Pile filling into drained tomatoes and replace
lids. Cling film and store in a cool place until
ready to serve.

PLANTAIN AND SWEET POTATO CRISPS

2¹/₂lb (1.1kg) plantain,
  peeled
2¹/₂lb (1.1kg) small
  sweet potatoes,
  peeled

oil for deep-frying
2 tbsp sea salt, crushed
  (optional)
pinch cayenne
  (optional)

S lice plantain into ¼″ (0.5cm) thick
slices and sweet potatoes into ⅛″
(0.3cm) thick slices.

Heat oil in a deep-fryer. Cook plantain
and sweet potato in separate batches until
golden and cooked through. Drain well on
kitchen paper.

Mix sea salt with cayenne and pour into a
greaseproof bag. Add vegetable chips and
shake them around until lightly coated.
Serve as soon as possible after cooking.

If preferred, the chips can be served
without salt and cayenne.

MUSHROOMS WITH PARMA HAM AND BASIL

*24 small open
  mushrooms*
2 tbsp olive oil
*2 tbsp finely chopped
  onion*
*6oz (175g) yellow
  pepper, diced*
*1 large clove garlic,
  crushed*
*2oz (50g) parma ham,
  diced*
6 black olives, chopped
*10 basil leaves,
  chopped*
2 tbsp pine kernels
*1½oz (40g) fresh white
  breadcrumbs*
seasoning

Remove stalks from mushrooms and chop them finely. Heat oil and cook onion gently until soft and translucent. Add mushroom stalks and yellow pepper, and cook until soft. Add remaining ingredients. Season. Remove from heat and allow filling to cool completely. Pack filling into mushroom caps and serve.

PINEAPPLE AND HAM PARCELS

*24 small spring roll
wrappers (from
Chinese
supermarkets)
oil for deep-frying*

*FILLING
1 tbsp finely chopped
spring onion
2oz (50g) mange-tout,
sliced across very
thinly
2oz (50g) pineapple
rings, chopped
4oz (100g) ham, cut
into thin strips
2 tsp soy sauce*

Blend together filling ingredients. Divide
between wrappers. Brush edges well
with water to seal and form into small
square parcels.

Heat oil and deep-fry rolls until crisp and
golden. Drain on kitchen paper and serve
while still hot.

CUCUMBER BOATS FILLED WITH PRAWNS AND TZATZIKI

3 cucumbers
salt
3 tbsp Greek yogurt
30 mint leaves, very
finely chopped

48 large cooked prawns
in their shell
dill sprigs

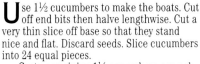

Use 1½ cucumbers to make the boats. Cut off end bits then halve lengthwise. Cut a very thin slice off base so that they stand nice and flat. Discard seeds. Slice cucumbers into 24 equal pieces.

Grate remaining 1½ cucumbers coarsely and sprinkle with salt. Leave in a colander for ½ hour or so. Rinse and drain well.

Place in a bowl and stir in yogurt and mint. Fill cucumber boats with this tzatziki mixture. Carefully peel the prawns and place 2 in each boat, tails overlapping edges. Top with sprigs of dill and serve.

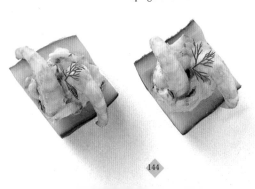

CELERY WITH RED CHEESE AND RADISH

6 sticks celery
3oz (75g) red vein
  cheddar, diced small

2 tbsp low-fat yogurt
6–8 radishes, thinly
  sliced

Wash celery and trim off ends. Cut a thin slice off base of each to make them stand nice and flat. Cut each stick into 4 equal pieces.

Mix diced cheese with yogurt. Divide the mixture between pieces of celery. Push radish slices into cheese mixture and serve.

PEPPERS WITH AUBERGINE AND PINE NUTS

5oz (150g) aubergine,
    diced
salt
4 tsp olive oil
I large clove garlic,
    crushed
pinch thyme
I tbsp pine kernels

4 tbsp Greek yogurt
2 tsp tahini paste
2 tbsp finely chopped
    parsley
seasoning
2–3 red or yellow
    peppers

Place diced aubergine in a colander and
sprinkle with salt. Leave for about ½
hour. Wash off salt and dry well on kitchen
paper.

Gently heat olive oil in a thick-bottomed
pan. Add aubergine and cook, stirring
frequently until soft. Add remaining filling
ingredients and continue cooking for a few
more minutes. Season. Remove from heat
and leave to cool.

Cut peppers along their lines, forming
natural divisions. Remove seeds, membranes
and stalks, and discard. Cut each section
across into halves.

Pile cold filling into pepper sections.
Cling film and store in a cool place until
ready to serve.

STUFFED AUBERGINE BAGUETTES

8 small thin aubergines
    (from Indian
    greengrocers)
oil for brushing

FILLING
2 tbsp olive oil
1 tbsp finely chopped
    onion
9oz (250g) skinned
    chicken breast fillet,
    diced small

1 tbsp pine kernels,
    coarsely chopped
2 tbsp finely chopped
    parsley
pinch rosemary
seasoning
6 black olives, chopped
1 small tomato, diced
    small

Heat oil in a frying pan. Add onion and cook gently until soft and golden. Add chicken and brown quickly. Lower heat and add remaining ingredients. Cook for a further couple of minutes.

Cut each aubergine into 3. Using an apple corer, remove centres and discard. Divide filling between aubergine pieces, brush surfaces with oil and place on a lightly oiled baking sheet. Cook in a preheated 190°C (375°F) Gas 5 oven for 20 minutes. Serve hot or cold.

MILD CHILLIES STUFFED WITH CHICKEN

24 mild Kenyan chillies,
  2–2½" (5–6cm)
  long
12oz (350g) skinned
  chicken fillet
3 tbsp cooking oil
2 cloves garlic, crushed
1 tbsp grated root
  ginger
4 tomatoes, skinned
  and chopped
3 tbsp chopped
  coriander
seasoning

Cut a sliver from each chilli, large enough to enable seeds to be removed and chilli to be stuffed. Discard cut-out pieces of chilli.

Cut chicken into small dice. Heat oil in a pan, add chicken and cook, stirring all the time, for 3–4 minutes. Add garlic, ginger and tomatoes. Cook briefly, then remove from heat. Stir in coriander and seasoning.

Fill chillies with chicken mixture. Place on a baking sheet and cook in a preheated 150°C (300°F) Gas 2 oven for 10 minutes. Serve hot or cold.

STUFFED MANGE-TOUT

24 large mange-tout,
   approx. 2oz (50g)
8oz (225g) white crab
   meat
3 tbsp quark
grated rind and juice ½
   lemon
1 heaped tbsp chopped
   chervil
seasoning
cayenne

Wash mange-tout. Plunge into salted, boiling water and blanch for a minute or so. Refresh in cold water. Trim off leafy ends with scissors. Carefully slit pods at curved edge (not one where peas are) and open just centre of pod.

Mix all ingredients for filling. Season. Fill pods with the mixture. Just before serving sprinkle over a very little cayenne.

MUSHROOMS WITH GARLIC SNAILS

24 medium button
  mushrooms, approx.
  14oz (400g)
4floz (100ml) olive oil
4floz (100ml) lemon
  juice

grated rind 1 lemon
seasoning
2oz (50g) soft butter
2 cloves garlic, crushed
1 tbsp very finely
  chopped parsley
24 canned snails

Carefully remove mushroom stalks (add to a soup or fry and eat on toast).

Blend together oil, lemon juice and rind, and season. Pour over mushrooms and leave to marinate for 1 hour or so, gently turning the mushrooms from time to time.

Blend together butter, garlic and parsley. Drain mushrooms. Place a small knob of garlic butter inside each mushroom and top with a snail.

Place mushrooms on a foil-lined baking sheet and cook in a preheated 200°C (400°F) Gas 6 oven for 5–6 minutes. Serve hot or warm.

SWEETCORN WRAPPED IN BACON

24 baby sweetcorn
12 slices streaky bacon,
   approx. 10oz (275g)

oil for brushing
1–2 tbsp paprika

Wash sweetcorn. Plunge into boiling salted water and blanch for 3–4 minutes. Refresh in cold water and dry on kitchen paper.

Remove rind from bacon and cut each slice in half lengthwise. Roll a bacon strip round each sweetcorn, leaving tips uncovered. Secure end of bacon strip with a cocktail stick.

Brush tips with a little oil, sprinkle with paprika and place sweetcorn on a foil-lined grill pan. Grill under medium heat until bacon is cooked, turning frequently and brushing tips with oil as required. Serve hot or cold.

ARTICHOKES WITH LEEK AND MUSHROOM

24 artichoke bottoms,
   approx. 4×14oz
   (400g) cans
3oz (75g) leeks, sliced
   very thinly
6oz (175g) mushrooms,
   sliced
1½oz (40g) butter
1oz (25g) plain flour

8floz (225ml) milk
2oz (50g) lean ham,
   chopped
2oz (50g) grated
   parmesan
pinch nutmeg
seasoning
chopped parsley

Line a roasting tray with foil. Place artichoke bottoms on it, trimming bases a little if necessary, so that they stand flat.

Dry leeks and mushrooms well on kitchen paper. Heat butter in a pan. Add vegetables and cook until soft and excess liquid evaporated. Stir in flour and cook a little longer. Remove from heat.

Heat milk until almost boiling. Add gradually to vegetable mixture, stirring all the time. Cook for a couple of minutes. Remove from heat, and add ham, parmesan and nutmeg. Season.

Spoon filling into artichoke bottoms. Cook in a preheated 200°C (400°F) Gas 6 oven for 15 minutes. Garnish with parsley and serve either warm or cold – if serving cold, cling film and store in a cool place until ready to serve.

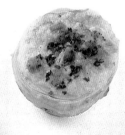

SPINACH PATTIES

PATTIES
10oz (275g) cooked
*   spinach, drained*
*   weight*
1 egg, beaten
4oz (100g) fresh
*   breadcrumbs*
1oz (25g) grated
*   cheese, preferably*
*   gruyère*

pinch marjoram
pinch nutmeg
salt to taste
a little oil for frying

TOPPING
4floz (100ml) soured
*   cream*
4oz (100g) lean bacon,
*   diced small*

Chop spinach finely and mix with all other ingredients. Shape into 24 small flat patties.

   Heat oil in a frying pan over medium heat and fry patties until lightly golden. Drain on kitchen paper.

   Top patties with 1 tsp soured cream. Crisp-fry bacon and sprinkle over patties. Serve hot or cold.

ASPARAGUS AND SALMON PÂTÉ EN CROUTE

24 slices white bread
3 tbsp cooking oil
5oz (150g) ready-made
* smoked salmon pâté*
2 tbsp soured cream

squeeze lemon juice
48 asparagus tips
salt
3 tbsp mint jelly
1 tbsp tarragon vinegar

Line 24 small rectangular pastry cases with bread slices. Trim edges with scissors, brush with oil and bake in a preheated 220°C (425°F) Gas 7 oven for 10 minutes. Leave to cool.

Blend pâté with soured cream and lemon juice. Set aside.

Blanch asparagus tips in salted water until just done. Refresh in cold water and drain well. Spoon pâté mixture into bread cases. Place 2 asparagus tips on top of pâté.

Melt mint jelly with vinegar and brush a very thin layer over asparagus spears to glaze. Cling film and store in a cool place until ready to serve.

DEEP-FRIED POTATO SKINS WITH TARAMA DIP

16 very large potatoes
vegetable oil for deep-frying

DIP
9floz (250ml) Greek yogurt
4floz (100ml) taramosalata
2 tbsp very finely chopped dill

Blend together yogurt, taramosalata and dill. Cling film and refrigerate while cooking potato skins.

Scrub potatoes very well and rinse in several changes of water. Cut out any blemishes in skins. Using a potato peeler, peel lengthwise in long, thin strips. (Reserve peeled potatoes and use in a gratin or other dish.) Rinse potato skins and dry thoroughly on kitchen paper.

Heat oil in a deep-fryer, and cook skins until crisp and golden. Drain on kitchen paper and serve as soon as possible after cooking, with the tarama dip.

FRESH DATES WITH PECAN AND RICOTTA

24 large fresh dates
3oz (75g) ricotta
20 pecan nuts, chopped
1 tbsp chopped chives

Cut a slit lengthwise in each date and remove stone carefully. Place ricotta in a bowl and stir in other ingredients.

Fill dates with cheese mixture. Cling film and store in a cool place until serving.